The Full Bag of Chips

IRELAND AND THE TRIPLE CROWN

PETER O'REILLY is the rugby correspondent of *The Sunday Tribune*. He has been reporting on rugby since the sport went professional in 1995. He lives in Dublin with Cliodhna and their two children, Lucy and Michael. This is his first book.

THE FULL BAG OF CHIPS

IRELAND AND THE TRIPLE CROWN

PETER O'REILLY

THE O'BRIEN PRESS
DUBLIN

First published 2004 by The O'Brien Press Ltd,
20 Victoria Road, Dublin 6, Ireland.
Tel: +353 1 4923333; Fax: +353 1 4922777
E-mail: books@obrien.ie
Website: www.obrien.ie

ISBN: 0-86278-897-8

British Library Cataloguing-in-Publication Data
O'Reilly, Peter
The Full Bag of Chips: Ireland and the Triple Crown
1.Rugby football - Tournaments - Ireland
2.Rugby football - Tournaments - Great Britain
3.Rugby Union football - Ireland
I.Title
796.3'33'09417

1   2   3   4   5   6   7   8   9   10
04   05   06   07   08   09   10

PHOTOGRAPH CREDITS

The author and publisher thank the following
for permission to use photographs in this book:
Inpho pages 32, 35, 42,
47, 53, 57, 63, 68, 77, 78, 79, 86, 89, 95, 100, 101, 104,
115, 116, 119, colour section; *The Irish Times* p40-1.
Cover photographs: Inpho

Typesetting, editing, layout and design: The O'Brien Press Ltd
Printing: Betaprint

CONTENTS

DEDICATION

In memory of John McCall (1985-2004)

ACKNOWLEDGEMENTS

Many thanks to Eddie O'Sullivan and the Triple Crown winners who kindly agreed to be interviewed: Brian O'Driscoll, Gordon D'Arcy, Girvan Dempsey, Shane Byrne, Reg Corrigan, Ronan O'Gara, Anthony Foley, Malcolm O'Kelly and Mike Ford; other most helpful interviewees were Des O'Brien, Jim McCarthy, Ciaran Fitzgerald, Ollie Campbell, Hugo MacNeill, Michael Bradley, Clive Woodward, Lawrence Dallaglio and Fergal O'Gara. Special thanks to John Redmond for his assistance and insight, also to Brian O'Brien; to Pat Fitzgerald for his generosity; to Martin Murphy and Joan Breslin of the IRFU for their help; also to Michael Cunningham and to Lindsey Hayes. The book could not have been written without the help of statisticians/historians like Willow Murray and John Griffiths. Special thanks are due to Des Daly and Frank Quinn of the *Irish Rugby Review* for permission to reproduce the statistics in the appendix. Karl Johnston, Ned van Esbeck and Sean Diffley were also very generous in allowing me to pilfer information from the books they have written about Irish rugby. Thanks to Tom, Bren, George and Billy for their help and advice; also to everyone at O'Brien Press. Finally, hugs and kisses to Cliodhna for all her love and encouragement.

PROLOGUE

Fergal O'Gara glanced anxiously at his watch and saw that it was time to go. If only the game wasn't locked at 10–10, it would be easier to budge the two young boys sitting either side of him in the front row of the upper west stand. They studiously ignored his signal, kept leaning forward, their hands tucked deep in their coat pockets, their eyes trained on the pitch. The younger one felt his cheeks redden slightly in frustration. Surely they could afford another couple of minutes. Just this once.

His dad wasn't all that happy about having to leave early himself. The script for the day was for Ireland to romp to their second Triple Crown within the space of three years. It was 1985. The team was led by Ciaran Fitzgerald – the same Ciaran Fitzgerald he had played alongside at UCG a decade previously. Now, at 10–10, the atmosphere at Lansdowne Road was impossibly tense. There was a routine to be followed, however. Fergal knew that if they were to make the 4.50pm train to Cork from Heuston Station, they had to be on the platform at Lansdowne Road Station before 4.00pm, and that meant leaving their seats around five minutes before the final whistle. With an eight-year-old and a nine-year-old in tow, you couldn't afford to get caught up in the beery-breathed crush heading down the concrete steps and into the tunnel at the base of the stand.

Colin and Ronan O'Gara knew the routine from experience. The day began early, the train to Dublin pulling out of Ceannt Station at 7.30 in the morning. On the way up, they'd talk about rugby. About how Ollie Campbell had been in Temple Hill a few weeks earlier to give a coaching clinic to the Cork Con under-10s and under-12s. About how he'd played on the last Ireland team to win a Triple Crown. He wore Adidas boots. Paul Dean wore Puma. And on and on. It was hungry work. The first port of call in Dublin was Bewley's on Grafton Street for a late breakfast. From there, it was a slow walk down the street to McDonald's for early lunch – they were better off indoors, for Dublin had been drenched that morning. Then Dad would take them along St Stephen's Green to the Shelbourne Hotel, where he'd have a pint with some of his friends from university. It was uncomfortable inside the hotel, stuffy and noisy. Where else would you be, though? The Irish team were staying here. Had they left for the game yet?

The excitement of anticipation had been excruciatingly sweet. Yet now, here they were, just as it was coming to the best bit, standing on the platform at Lansdowne Road railway station. Was it still 10–10? As the filthy orange diesel groaned its way out of the station, word went round that Rob Andrew, the English out-half, had just missed a penalty. The train was packed, standing-room only, mostly Cork accents. But only one voice could be heard in the O'Garas' carriage – that of Jim Sherwin, RTÉ Radio's match commentator. One of the 4.50pm regulars had had the good sense to bring a transistor radio and soon everyone in the carriage was listening hard. As the train trundled towards the city centre, half a mile away at Lansdowne Road came the sequence that would be played and replayed – Brian Spillane gathering Fitzgerald's throw at the tail of a line-out, Donal Lenihan charging towards the England posts. Once Michael Kiernan slotted into the out-half position, Sherwin sensed the inevitability of it all and delivered a description that was simple yet apt – 'Drop-goal on. Drop-goal taken. Drop-goal good!'

The reactions in the carriage were rather more primal. 'Pandemonium,' recalls Fergal O'Gara. 'My first thought was for the boys' safety, because for a second I thought the carriage was going to derail. I still get slagged about missing the Triple Crown moment. We all had to watch the Kiernan drop-goal on video later on. It's funny, though. In hindsight, you remember things more vividly because you weren't there.'

Ronan O'Gara has heard the story repeated so often that he feels as though he can remember every syllable of Sherwin's commentary. For others in Ireland's 2004 team, the memories are less distinct. Victor Costello was standing on the south terrace that day – at fourteen, he was already over six feet tall, a member of the Blackrock College Junior Cup Team and well able to handle the human tidal wave triggered by Kiernan's drop-goal. But Costello was the only member of the 2004 team at Lansdowne Road that day.

Reggie Corrigan would have been there but for Uncle Benedict's wedding in Galway. He has vague recollections of being in a hotel bar watching the game on television, of how the menfolk were reluctant to move despite urgings to go into the function room for dinner. Anthony Foley reckons he was watching the television in the family pub in Killaloe but he has clearer memories of the 1982 Triple Crown – his father, Brendan, had played for Ireland earlier that season. As for the other thirty-somethings in the 2004 team, Shane Byrne says he probably watched it in the junior common room in Blackrock with the other boarders, but he can't be sure. Malcolm O'Kelly remembers how England were massive underdogs for the final game but, again, has no detailed recollection. And John Hayes? As he puts it, if you'd shown him a rugby ball back in 1985, he'd have assumed it was a Gaelic football that had been run over by a car.

The others – the likes of Brian O'Driscoll, Geordan Murphy or Gordon D'Arcy – are too young to remember very much at all about the year 1985, let alone the Triple Crown. Truth be told, it's not a phrase that would have had much currency with any of the players coming into the 2004 Six Nations. Ireland didn't enter the championship seeking 'an elusive seventh crown'.

The Triple Crown, already an imaginary prize, had become more illusive than elusive, something associated with an era when rugby balls still had laces. The Rugby World Cup was primarily to blame. Back in 1985, when a global tournament was still just an idea being pushed by New Zealand and Australia, the Five Nations was the be-all and end-all. The French might have been miffed about the idea of the Triple Crown, but they'd joined the party late, so they'd just have to put up with it. The advent of the Rugby World Cup in 1987 changed everything. Suddenly, here was the tournament which decided a country's true position in the game's pecking order. By the time Italy made it the Six Nations in 2000, the Triple Crown was practically an anachronism – it might even have been dismissed as such had anyone bothered to mention it. It wasn't mentioned because nobody had won it since 1990 except England and it wasn't important to them. England, the worst team in the championship back in 1985, now dealt in bigger currencies – Grand Slams and World Cups only, please.

Not surprisingly then, when Ireland had the temerity to win at Twickenham on 6 March 2004, there was rather more emphasis placed on the fact that they had beaten the world champions than on the prospect of winning a Triple Crown. RTÉ's Clare MacNamara made the first media reference to the mythical prize in her post-match interview with Eddie O'Sullivan. The Ireland coach admitted that the Triple Crown hadn't crossed his mind. It was a 'good two hours after the final whistle before someone in the press room mentioned the words and, even then, very few hacks stopped to consider the significance. Ireland had just beaten England. That was the story. And in the dressing room? 'It might have been mentioned in some corner at some stage,' says Corrigan. 'But everything was such a blur.'

It wasn't until the following Tuesday morning that it became an issue. As usual, O'Sullivan's first team meeting of the week was in 'The Bunker', the video analysis room on the third floor of the Citywest Hotel, which serves as the players' second home during every international season. Triple Crown talk was done and dusted in about five minutes. There was to be no further mention of it that week, O'Sullivan said. The media would make a meal of it but the job was to beat Italy the following Saturday. So it was shrugged off in press conferences that week – and the next. In order to keep the focus sharp, O'Sullivan feigned something approaching indifference in response to any question related to 1985 and the players followed his example.

Subsequently, however, they would admit it was impossible not to be affected by the hype. And, in a way, they wanted to be affected by it, wanted it to be considered something special, wanted to be part of a team set apart. It was, according to Byrne, a pain in the arse that Ireland never won anything. Sure, O'Driscoll and Donncha O'Callaghan had under-19 World Cup medals. A few others had won an under-21 Triple Crown, the likes of David Wallace and Girvan Dempsey. But the senior team? A World Cup quarter-final and the odd one-off result – that was it. A Triple Crown suddenly became mighty attractive. Ireland had won only six in over a century. Wales had won seventeen, Scotland ten. What they wouldn't give for one now. Anachronism? No. By the time Scotland arrived in Dublin in the final weekend of March, there was something major at stake. Ireland were playing, as O'Sullivan would put it, for 'the full bag of chips'.

CHAPTER I – THE TRIPLE CROWN

HEN'S TEETH

Contrary to popular belief, there *is* a Triple Crown trophy. It's kept in the Museum of Rugby at Twickenham. It's an odd-looking thing, around 450 millimetres tall, and carved out of ... coal. The catalogue may describe it as 'burnished anthracite' but that doesn't stop it being a lump of coal hewn from the Haig Colliery in Cumbria in 1975. A retired miner by the name of Dave Marrington got to work with his penknife and turned it into a surprisingly ornate work, with a crown (surprise, surprise) sitting on a four-sided base on which are represented a rose, a shamrock, a thistle and the Prince of Wales feathers.

It ain't pretty. Tudor Jones liked it, though. Jones was sports editor of *Coal News,* a weekly publication with a circulation of just under half a million readers across the UK in the mid-70s. Tudor thought Marrington's creation was an appropriate prize for a Crown-winning team (in those days, that only meant Wales) and waged a campaign to have it accepted by officialdom. He lugged the thing to Edinburgh, Twickenham and Dublin, and wrote prolifically on the subject. He received polite rejection slips from all four home unions. He tried to enlist the support of Welsh players but had no joy. As he wrote: 'Gareth [Edwards] and Gerald [Davies] have told me that they preserve, even protect, the Triple Crown myth. They see beauty in their piece of rugby make-believe. I have no wish to spoil their dream either. After all, they are miners' sons, proud and true, to the roots. In a nice way, I can keep my coal.' Nice try, Tudor.

As to the provenance of the name 'Triple Crown', no-one is altogether sure, though it's generally assumed that a journalist is responsible. Several rugby histories state that it was first used in the *South Wales Daily News*, a forerunner of the *Western Mail*, on 20 March 1899. In fact, *The Irish Times* got there at least five years earlier. Witness the introduction to the newspaper's Ireland v Wales match report on Monday, 12 March 1894: 'After long years of seemingly hopeless struggle Ireland has achieved the triple crown honours of Rugby football. For the first time in the annals of the game have the Hibernians proved beyond cavil or doubt their right to be dubbed champions of the nations and that the Irishmen fully deserve the great distinction no one will deny ...' Hurrah for Hibernia!

We'll probably never know whether this is the first written reference to the Triple Crown. It doesn't really matter. It's a wizard place to start.

1894

It's appropriate to use the *Irish Times* archives as a source for anything to do with Irish rugby in the 'gay '90s'. Rugby was primarily a game for the Protestant middle class, whose attitudes were reflected by that newspaper. The only Catholic in Edmund Forrest's 1894 team was Tom Crean – no relation to the famous explorer – who had been educated by the Jesuits at Clongowes Wood and who went on to earn the Victoria Cross for services rendered to the British Empire in the Boer War.

Of the eighteen players used in the three games, thirteen were from three Dublin clubs – Wanderers, Dublin University and Bective Rangers – and the remaining five were from Ulster. They had a variety of occupations: doctors, clergymen, a university lecturer, a detective, an auctioneer, a solicitor, merchants and company directors. When, on Monday, 12 March, the Dublin contingent opened their *Irish Times*, their eyes might briefly have been distracted by advertisements for department stores like Clery's, Switzer's, McBirney's and Brown Thomas. They would have skipped over the ad for Congreve's Balsamic Elixir ('The World's Grand Remedy'), but maybe paused to read a forecast of Queen Victoria's speech for the opening of parliament. The editorial writer believed 'things in Ireland' had improved considerably since Mr Gladstone had been removed from office

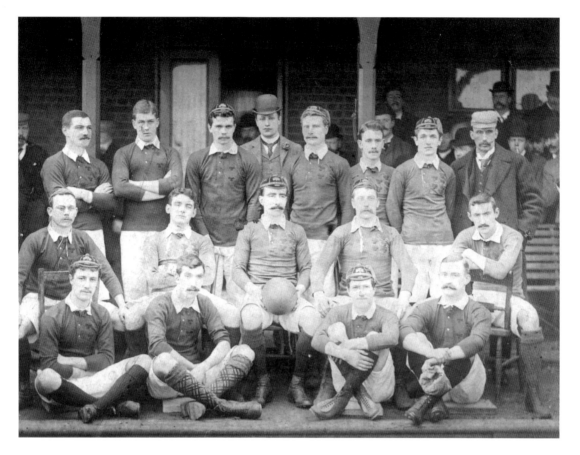

The Ireland team that beat England 7–5 at Blackheath, 3 February 1894. *Back row*: James Lytle, Tom Crean, Harry Lindsay, R Garrett (President, IRFU), Charles Rooke, Walter Brown, Lucius Gwynn, E McAlister (Honorary Secretary, IRFU); *Seated*: Bertie Wells, Willie Gardiner, Edmund Forrest (captain), John O'Conor, Sam Lee; *Front*: Ben Tuke, George Walmsley, William Sparrow, Jack Lytle.

for the fourth and, given his failing health, surely the last time. This, he assumed, would be the end of that Home Rule nonsense. Eventually, on page five, the reader would find a lively report on events in Ballynafeigh, Belfast, the previous Saturday.

You need to use your imagination to get a picture of what rugby union was like in 1894. It's worth remembering that it was a relatively new sport. Ireland had played its first international game a mere nineteen years previously and this was only the eighth season they had fixtures against all three of the other 'home nations'. You have to wonder about the standard of organisation when it's reported that Ireland turned up two men short for their game in Cardiff in 1884 and had to borrow a couple of Welsh players. You have to wonder about the quality of the tackling when it emerges that D B Walkington, Ireland's full-back in the late 1880s, wore a monocle while playing. Scores were infrequent – Ireland's 'for and against' aggregate for their three victories in 1894 was just 15–5. It was, as Bective forward John O'Conor later recorded in his diary, attritional stuff:

'In those days, handling was not developed to the same extent that came later. The game was left almost entirely to the forwards and the scrums were grim affairs, with all their forwards giving full weight to the shove. There were no specialised positions such as hooker or wing forward, and every forward was expected to be an accomplished hooker. First up, first down was the rule. The backs were used mainly in defence.'

There were a couple of changes for the 1894 championship. For the first time, Ireland followed the Welsh model of using seven backs instead of six. The selection committee was reduced from ten to six, while this was also the first championship when referees were given full powers and no longer had to wait for appeals from players. Quite how much all of this had to do with Ireland winning the Triple Crown is uncertain. What's clear is that they weren't expected to win it.

Ireland were installed as 5/1 outsiders for the opener at Blackheath against England. They won 7–5 but left it late. Trailing 3–5 in the dying minutes, they had Forrest to thank for a late drop-goal, then worth four points. They left it late three weeks later at Lansdowne Road too, when Bective's winger Bertie Wells scored the decisive try against Scotland in front of a crowd of 10,000.

The championship was still at stake when Wales, the Triple Crown holders, arrived at the 'Ulster Cricket Club enclosure' following a 7–0 victory over Scotland in Newport. Our enthusiastic *Irish Times* correspondent reported that there was controversy even before kickoff: 'The occasion under notice was the first on which the Welsh match was played in Belfast and if the Taffies can possibly do anything to prevent it, it will be the last. The venue is by no means an ideal football ground and the visitors showed lively dissatisfaction with it, and before the commencement of the game entered a protest against the match being played. Their contention was that the ground was not of the required measurement, being some eight yards too narrow and six yards short of the standard dimensions, in addition to which they considered the corners bordering on the cinder track were decidedly dangerous.'

The rain of the preceding days had also left the surface sodden, forcing the club executive to start carrying out impromptu draining operations at six in the morning. But there was no thought of postponement – two Great Northern Company trains had brought 800 spectators from Dublin, which 'considerably augmented the company, which at the commencement of hostilities could not have been far short of 6,000 – a very respectable figure for Belfast, where the association game is most thought of'.

God love our saturated scribe, who produced an exhaustively descriptive account of what was, by common consent, a dreadful contest played in dire conditions. The game's one score came early and was described thus: 'Escott was quickly brought to book by the referee and as events proved, he cost his side the match. A "scrum" was being fought out midway between the Taffies' 25 and the line when the Cardiff half-back picked the ball out, for which, of course, Mr Rainie awarded Ireland a penalty free, and John Lyttle kicking a magnificent goal, the cheering was loud and prolonged.'

The anonymous writer maintained a degree of objectivity, noting that it was 'very tantalising to the Taffies' to lose by a solitary score. But fair is fair – 'We said the Hibernians were lucky to win but no-one will grudge them this slice of fortune's favour, remembering, as all footballers must, the cruel hard lines we have had in previous years.'

1899

Except for the skintight jerseys, the players of 1899 looked nothing like today's international players. Judging by old photographs, if you played for Ireland in the 1890s, there's a fair chance you had knobbly knees and an even better chance that a moustache decorated your upper lip. If you weighed all of fourteen stone – like Girvan Dempsey – then you were practically a behemoth. Just occasionally, however, strangely familiar characters emerge from the old match reports. From the 1894 team, for example, the outstanding back was Sam Lee of Northern Ireland Football Club (NIFC), described as 'low-slung, elusive and phenomenally strong'. Brian O'Driscoll's spiritual forefather, surely.

By the time of Ireland's next Triple Crown, in 1899, there were two brothers in the pack – Mick and Jack Ryan from the Rockwell College Club. They were from farming stock and bred horses for a living – Jack would train 100/1 outsider Tipperary Tim to victory in the 1928 Grand National. The Ryans were also prominent Gaelic footballers and international athletes, specialising in what would now be termed 'power events' – they wreaked havoc on the rugby pitch. According to the Welsh reporter Dromio (W J Townsend Collins), the Ryans were '... big, powerful, ruthless players who never struck me as really great footballers. They were of the same stamp as the Welsh forwards, Harry Day and Dick Hellings, more brawn than brain, but more deliberately aggressive than the Welshmen, with rather less concern for the consequences of their unrestrained exercises of strength.' Yes, it's Donncha O'Callaghan and Paul O'Connell.

By now, the names and phrases appearing in the *Irish Times* editorial page had historical resonance – Dreyfus, Kaiser Wilhelm, women's suffrage and, of course, Queen Victoria, now on her last legs. As for the Irish rugby team, there were no survivors from 1894 and there was a much higher player turnover during the championship. Twenty-four players were used in all, the Ryans being among the five who were picked for all three games. Unquestionably the most distinguished was Aloysius Mary 'Louis' Magee, a veterinary student in London, playing for London Irish but also with strong

Louis Magee's team before their 3-0 win over Wales in Cardiff on 18 March 1899. *Back row*: T M McGowan (IRFU Committee), Billy Byron, Mick Ryan, Jim Sealy, Jack Ryan, Cecil Moriarty, Arthur Meares, J B Moore (President, IRFU). *Seated*: Jack McIlwaine, Edward Campbell, Tommy Little, Magee, Gerald Allen, Carl Reid, George Harman. *Front*: Gerald 'Blucher' Doran, Pierce O'Brien-Butler.

Bective connections. Captain and half-back – in modern terms, a scrum-half – he played a significant part in four of Ireland's five tries that season.

The 'opening engagement', as the *Irish Times* put it, was against England at Lansdowne Road. By now there was even pre-match entertainment: 'The band of the King's Own Yorkshire Light Infantry will play selections of popular music before the game commences. Trams run every few minutes from the Pillar to within a few yards of the ground, while the train service from Westland Row is a capital one.' How jolly.

Those who made the trip saw Ireland win 6–0, their fourth win over England in succession. Two weeks later, it was off to Inverleith, where Magee's team scored a whopping total of three tries – only the third time they had achieved this. They won 9–3, the penalty goal scored by Scottish captain Bill Donaldson being the only score they would concede in the championship. The final game in Cardiff still reads like a tense affair, however.

The *Irish Times* either had a new rugby correspondent by this stage or else he'd become crusty in his old age. He didn't like the overcrowding at the Arms Park that day. 'In an hour, there were 20,000 spectators within the enclosure. By the thousand still they came, till at 2.30 a further 10,000 were within the enclosure. Then an untoward event occurred – on the popular side, the palissade gave way owing to the weight of the crowd and five or six hundred spectators rushed like a swarm of locusts through the breach, and, to continue the simile, they as effectively destroyed everything they touched … next, the Pressmen from all parts of the Three Kingdoms had to fly for their lives for fear of the terrible crush.' That crush was to cause numerous stoppages during the game, as Mick Ryan later described in the *Rockwell College Annual*: 'They crowded on the touch and goal lines and at times it seemed an impossibility for Ireland to score; as one reporter said afterward, "Wales had a thousand full-backs."'

Ireland did score before the break, however, through Lansdowne winger Gerald 'Blucher' Doran. Inevitably, they had to weather a storm in the second half, their tenacity epitomised by Magee's famous tackle on Skrimshire, the Welsh wing, right at the death. Again, Mick Ryan provides the description: 'Still Wales pinned us in our own 25 and it seemed as if nothing could prevent a score. And then came the most exciting incident of the game. Lloyd whisked the ball out to Nicholls. Straight through all opposition he went, swerved and transferred to Skrimshire, who seemed to have a perfectly clear field. He had lightning speed and there appeared to be nothing to prevent him scoring under the posts. Suddenly Magee flashed up and dived for his heels. Amidst frantic cheers from the Irish supporters, Skrimshire came down and lost the ball.' Definitely a Peter Stringer moment, by the sound of it. Ireland won 3–0.

1948

Consider for a moment the moral outrage and tabloid mayhem if, on the night of Ireland's 2004 Triple Crown triumph over Scotland, three players – say, Gordon D'Arcy, Reggie Corrigan and Anthony Foley – had ended up under lock and key in a police station for causing a public disturbance. Picture the headlines: 'RUGBY STARS' NIGHT OF SHAME', 'TRIPLE TROUBLE FOR RUGGER RENEGADES'. And so on. This is what happened on the night Ireland beat Wales in 1948 yet the incident – to be described in more detail later – was kept under wraps. Back then, sport and scandal mixed only occasionally. Besides, there was a much bigger story – Ireland had won the Triple Crown.

Karl Mullen's 1948 team is now referred to as the Grand Slam side but at the time the slam had no currency – it wasn't until later that the term was borrowed from tennis. The Five Nations was a fair way off too. In 1948, the competition's official title was the International Championship. France took part but they were still viewed with a degree of suspicion – for the eight seasons leading up to World War II, they had been excluded due to allegations of professionalism within their clubs. For Ireland to win the championship would be special (the last time this had happened was in 1935). To win a Triple Crown was practically unheard of – it hadn't happened in forty-nine years.

There were just two survivors from Louis Magee's team and one of them, Billy Byron from NIFC, was at Ravenhill for the decisive game in 1948. He even brought his 1899 jersey along as a good-luck charm and had his photograph taken with Mullen, Jim McCarthy and JC Daly just minutes before kickoff. It's a grey old photograph and these were grey old times. Less than three years after war had ended, rationing was still in operation, though less stringently enforced in Ireland than in the UK. When Ireland travelled to England, Scotland or Wales, the players often brought packages of goodies as gifts to exchange with their opposite numbers – like Haffner's sausages from Dublin, which actually contained real meat.

In such austere times, for a national team to achieve success brought a level of excitement that present-day sports fans might struggle to comprehend. For the majority, following the game meant listening to BBC Radio's Rex Alston. A sidekick commentator helped listeners picture the action by occasionally intoning the name of the quadrant in which the ball was situated, the pitch being composed of eight notional squares.

Part of the magic of this story is the sheer unpredictability of it all. The campaign could hardly be described as a triumph of careful planning or selectorial strategy. The previous year, Ireland had beaten England by 22–0 at Lansdowne Road – a record margin – yet the following December, they were trounced 16–3 by the touring Wallabies. There was no coach (that was still twenty years away) and team selection involved a degree of horse trading between the five selectors – two each from Leinster and Ulster, and one from Munster. It just wasn't done to question the selection. To ask, for example, why Ernie Strathdee, the Presbyterian minister from Queen's University who led Ireland to victory in Paris, was replaced by Harlequins' Hugh de Lacy for the next game, or why Garryowen centre Paddy Reid was dropped when Scotland came to Lansdowne Road. 'Back then, a selector was God and a player kissed every ass he had to,' recalled McCarthy, who had made his international debut in Paris. 'It didn't even occur to you to question why they travelled first class and you were in third. You had guys like Ernie Crawford, who did everything – he'd do touch judge and give the team talk beforehand. I was told early on to stay in his good books and I'd be well set.'

It may have been by chance but the selectors got certain things right. After that victory in Paris, they handed the captaincy to Karl Mullen, a medical student from Old Belvedere. At 21, Mullen was the youngest player on the side but he was a thoughtful, inspirational leader, and a top-class hooker. Crawford and his cronies also hit upon a magical formula in the back row. Bill McKay, a 400-metre runner and Ulster boxing champion, was a 'veteran' of the previous year's championship, the first after the war. If he was the enforcer, McCarthy was the support player, astonishingly light on his feet and with an uncanny prescience for the movements of Jack

Karl Mullen's Grand Slam squad of 1948. *Back row*: Ernie Crawford (touch judge), Des McKee, Jim McCarthy, JC Daly, Jimmy Nelson, Colm Callan, Des O'Brien, Jim McKay, Bertie O'Hanlon, M Allen (referee). *Seated*: Bertie McConnell, Barney Mullan, Karl Mullen (captain), Dr T M McGrath (President, IRFU), Dudley Higgins, Paddy Reid. *Front*: Mick O'Flanagan (superimposed), Ernie Strathdee, Jack Mattsson (superimposed), Jack Kyle, Hugh de Lacy (superimposed). Insets: Ernie Keeffe, Jim Corcoran, Bob Agar.

Kyle, the out-half and the team's real star. Finally there was Des O'Brien, the 28-year-old from London Irish who won his first cap at Twickenham. An international at squash and hockey, he was also a free-roaming number eight who completed one of rugby's finest back rows. O'Brien recalled: 'In those years we played for Ireland, none of us had a wife, let alone a motor car. We either walked or cycled. It gave us a natural fitness which players don't have today.'

It was a different game. A try was worth three points and a drop-goal four (though this was reduced to three in 1949). In the scrums, the hooker would launch himself into the second row of the opposing pack to compete for the ball. It was still the era of the foot-rush. Defending back lines weren't required to stand ten yards behind the line-out, while the offside line was at the middle of the scrum. This made Kyle's elusiveness all the more remarkable, and made McCarthy appear to be in a perpetual state of offside. When the offside law was changed in the early 1950s, they said it was because of McCarthyism.

If Computacentre, the statisticians employed by the Six Nations, had been recording the stats in 1948, they would have listed a lot of scrums and line-outs and lots of kicking from the hand. Ireland played a simple but effective game, illuminated only on occasions by Kyle's genius. 'Kyle didn't do a lot but he'd make two or three ferocious breaks and that was it,' said O'Brien. 'The plan was largely to hold the ball for the first twenty minutes, not give it to Kyle at all and then release him. That was one tactic we used anyway. It wasn't as though we went in for video analysis. We weren't allowed meet until twenty-four hours before kickoff. I remember before my first cap, we were on our way to our Friday training session at the Duke of York Barracks on the outskirts of London. Karl came down to me and asked me to lead the pack the following day. I said I couldn't. I hardly knew any of the others because I'd been based in London since '41. But he insisted, and took me around the bus, introducing me to Jim McCarthy and Billy McKay. Extraordinary when you think of it. But Karl was a shrewd operator, a great player and a very encouraging captain. If I recall correctly, he was the first captain to go in for a team talk. He simplified things. He knew our strengths. He didn't go in for flashy back play. We had Kyle and this very fit back row.'

While Karl Mullen provided tactical acumen and common sense, John Christopher Daly offered irreverence. The 32-year-old prop from Cobh was tall, dark, dashing and had a cavalier approach to rugby and to life. 'An extraordinary character,' said O'Brien. 'Before the war, Daly was playing for

London Irish thirds just for fun. When the war broke out, he joined London Irish Rifle Brigades. He pinched a ball and said, "I'll be back after the war to play for Ireland." He'd been a telephone pointsman in London so he was made a type of sherpa for a wireless operator on the front line, in northern African and in Italy. He had some exciting times. When he got back after five years, he was also immensely strong. He'd been carrying two or three hundredweight on his back nearly all that time. He was fit as a flea. Before internationals he would do double back somersaults to confirm it.'

As it happened, Daly returned from injury for the trip to London – the first aeroplane flight for the majority of the team. It was a game Ireland should have won a lot more easily than the 11–10 score line suggests. The story of the day was the missed penalty by Barney Mullan, the Clontarf wing, early in the second half. 'If he'd got that, we were out of sight at 14–5,' said McCarthy. 'Instead, he hit the upright, and the ball ends up in the hands of Dicky Guest, their wing. He runs up to our full-back, Jack Mattsson, gives him the old twinklers and scores under the posts. We got home but it was piss-in-your-trousers stuff.'

Ireland had won their two away games and were now firmly fancied to beat Scotland at Lansdowne Road on 28 February. They duly won 6–0 thanks to tries by Mullan and Kyle. And so to Ravenhill. Ravenhill? Yes, Ulster was Leinster's equal in terms of power on the IRFU committee and so demanded a home international, even if the ground's capacity was no more than 30,000.

Ireland had home advantage but Wales were clear favourites. Bleddyn Williams was the best centre in the world and Ken Jones, an Olympic sprinter, was one of the game's quickest wings. The man Ireland concentrated on mostly, though, was Haydn Tanner, the irrepressible Cardiff scrum-half known as 'The Master'. Ireland knew that to get to Wales, they needed to get to Tanner first. O'Brien was given the job. Tanner was buried twice in the first ten minutes, once with the ball, once without. He was quiet after that.

The scores were level 3–3 at half-time, Williams sidestepping over to

A match ticket for Ireland's 'Grand Slam' game against Wales in 1948 in Belfast. It cost sixpence more to pay at the gate – if you could get in. Ravenhill was packed to its 30,000 capacity.

cancel Barney Mullan's thirteenth-minute try. Ireland were winning the forward battle, however, with Karl Mullen wreaking havoc on the Welsh put-in. He received a pummelling for his efforts but convinced his players that all they needed was patience. O'Brien recalled: 'Karl told us that if we could just score once more and hold on, we'd be remembered for the rest of our lives. He was right.'

The main target of Ireland's second-half offensive was Frank Trott, the Welsh full-back and an undertaker by profession. He was subjected to an unmerciful bombardment by Kyle and it was his error, seven minutes into the second half, that was decisive. O'Brien and Daly latched on to Trott's spillage, hoofing it 30 metres over the Welsh try-line for Daly to get the touchdown. Half an hour later, naked from the waist up, he was being

Menu	*Toasts*
MUTTON BROTH	*His Majesty the King*
SCALLOPS A LA MORNAY	*The Welsh Team*
	Proposed by Mr. T. M. McGRATH, M.D. (President, Irish Rugby Football Union)
ROAST TURKEY	*Response by* G. H. TANNER (Captain of Wales)
SAUSAGE	
GREEN PEAS ROAST POTATOES	*The Irish Team*
PLUM PUDDING	*Proposed by* Mr. T. H. VILE (Vice-President, Welsh Rugby Football Union)
BRANDY SAUCE	*Response by* C. MULLEN (Captain of Ireland)
MARASCHINO ICE	*The Referee*
	Proposed by Mr. G. P. S. HOGAN, B.L. (Vice-President, Irish Rugby Football Union)
COFFEE	*Response by* Mr. MALCOLM ALLEN

The menu card for the meal Des O'Brien found so unimpressive on the night Ireland secured the Grand Slam. Note that Karl Mullen is C Mullen – they would get his initial right from this point on.

chaired off the field by an hysterical crowd – souvenir hunters had torn the jersey from his back.

The most popular story from that day is how Daly's jersey was cut into tiny pieces to be sold as 'holy' relics, some of which can, supposedly, still be found on mantelpieces in remote parts of Ireland. More remarkable is what happened later that evening in Belfast. Somewhat surprisingly, there were no official celebrations planned and the attempts of a few players to find entertainment led them into trouble. 'I suppose it was because we weren't expected to win,' said O'Brien. 'We hadn't won one in so long. There was tremendous excitement about it but it was seen as most unlikely that we'd do it. So all we had was another mangy dinner.' This took place at Thompson's restaurant in Donegall Place (the menu for the evening is printed above). However, the bar at the Grand Central Hotel closed at ten o'clock that evening, so O'Brien headed off in search of diversion with Daly, Reid and Derek Monteith, who had captained Ireland the previous season. There was a dance in Queen's University but it finished at midnight, just ten minutes after the Triple Crown heroes arrived. It was as they were walking back towards the hotel that they encountered trouble, in the shape of an Orange flute band, which, for some reason, had chosen that Saturday night to go marching. The sight of the band marching around the corner clearly irked one of the four, who rushed towards the Orangemen, his fists flailing.

'We thought we'd better rescue him, so we waded in after him,' recalled O'Brien. 'I can still see the boys with the big Lambegs, taking the drums off their shoulders and coming in around us. I was sure we were about to get done. There were blows struck. In Glasgow, they would have called it a "real rammie". We must have been close to a police station because we were hauled out, arms twisted behind our backs, run along a pavement, through swing doors and into a police station. There was one sergeant there, who chucked us into a cell. We weren't very upset as I recall.'

All except Monteith, a northern Protestant and a lawyer by profession. After much hammering on the cell door, he was released at around two o'clock to plead on his friends' behalf. 'Half an hour later we were marched out into the guard room, where there were about twenty RUC men standing in two rows with their hands behind their backs. We were lectured by the sergeant, who said something along the lines of "Try that again, and there will be no more Triple Crowns for you boys." Then they let us go. It must have been 3.30 before we got to our beds. Not a word to anyone, of course.'

For Daly, the excitement was only beginning. By the time the southern-ers' train arrived back in Amiens Street the following afternoon, a huge crowd had gathered to welcome the heroes. Daly was whisked off in a sports car by a girl he had never met but who was sporting a piece of his jersey on her blouse. 'He shacked up with her for a whole week and lost his job when he got back to London,' said O'Brien. 'That's why he accepted an offer from Huddersfield to play rugby league.'

As for O'Brien, he missed the joyous scenes at Amiens Street because he had taken the earlier at train, at 7.30am from Belfast. A pressing engagement? 'Yes, I had a hockey game in Crumlin at two o'clock on the Sunday afternoon, for Guinness Park Royal [the London brewery] against Guinness Dublin. It just so happened that that the Park Royal jersey was green so I proudly wore my Ireland rugby jersey that day.'

1949

The '49ers will always remain in the shadow of the previous year's team and it's not hard to see why. The '48 side was the first Irish one to win a Triple Crown in the twentieth century. Winning another crown the following year was exceptional yet, somehow, it didn't seem to catch the public imagination in quite the same way. Des O'Brien remembers a lot for an octogenarian but he doesn't remember there being a huge fuss when the boat carrying the team docked at Dún Laoghaire after the decisive win in Swansea. Maybe it was just that the players got used to winning. Between 1948 and 1951, Ireland played 17 games, won 11, drew two and lost just four – unprecedented success.

The '49ers were probably a better team, however. 'There had been awful messing at scrum-half and centre the previous year,' said Jim McCarthy. 'This time the selectors eventually settled on Ernie Strathdee to partner Jack [Kyle] and they brought in Noel Henderson at centre. He was a real find. We also had Tom Clifford to come in for JC Daly. When you get into a winning team, it almost never dawns on you that you'll be beaten. That's the way we were at that stage.'

Crucially, the team was provided with a specialist place-kicker in fullback George Norton of Bective Rangers. 'George was a very good, old-fashioned full-back – a solid fielder, a long kicker, good tackler,' said O'Brien. 'He was probably the first Irishman who went out sedulously and practised place-kicking for two or three hours twice a week. He used to go down to Bective with a bag of balls and get a young lad to throw them back to him. Nobody had done that before.' It showed too. Whereas Ireland had managed the grand total of three successful kicks at goal during the 1948 Grand Slam, Norton now established a new Irish record with 26 points in the championship.

Norton didn't have the best start to his international career, against France at Lansdowne Road, a game Ireland lost 9–16. From there, Ireland's forwards were utterly dominant over England and Scotland, games Ireland won 14–5 and 13–3, with McCarthy scoring two tries against the Scots. There merely remained a trip to Swansea, where Ireland hadn't won since 1889. Extra ships were called into service to ferry the huge Irish support across the Irish Sea. A stand ticket would have set you back 10 shillings (at the time a loaf of bread cost half a shilling).

It was, by all accounts, a poor game but O'Brien's recollections convey a

The team that won a second consecutive Triple Crown in Swansea on 12 March 1949. Bill McKay (second from right, back row) was a doubtful starter until his arrival in St Helen's minutes before kick-off. *Back row*: C R Graves (touch judge), Mick Lane, Tom Clifford, Des McKee, Leslie Griffin, Des O'Brien, Jimmy Nelson, George Norton, Bill McKay, Tom Pearce (referee). *Seated*: Jim McCarthy, Bob Agar, Karl Mullen (captain) G P S Hogan (President, IRFU), Bertie O'Hanlon, Noel Henderson. Front: Jack Kyle, Ernie Strathdee.

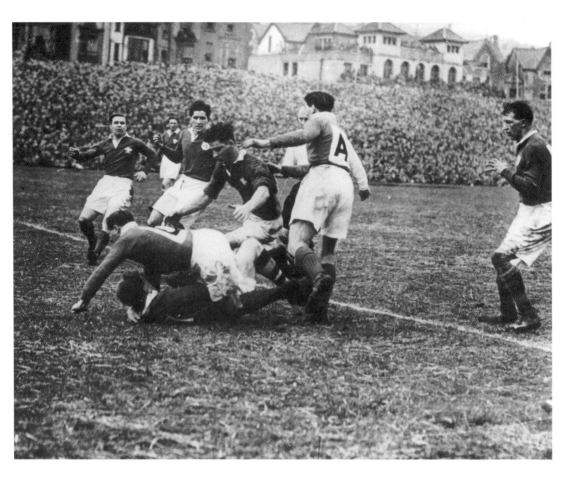

Having chased Jack Kyle's kick, Jim McCarthy gets the all-important try at Swansea in 1949. It was another moment to forget for Welsh full-back, Frank Trott (lying on the prone McCarthy).

certain tension, especially during the build-up. 'Our main problem was with the touch flags,' said O'Brien. 'One of the touchlines at Swansea runs at an angle to the spectators and they had touch flags that were only two feet high. It was very deceptive, especially for a full-back. Karl Mullen protested strongly to Tom Pearce, the English referee, and eventually they got replacements. Then there was a big worry over Bill McKay, who was arriving late after doing an exam in Belfast and got caught up in traffic. Terry Davis of Trinity was put into his jersey. But McKay arrived ten minutes before kickoff and poor Terry never got a cap.'

O'Brien got a knock on his knee just before half-time and had to hobble his way through the second half – there was no such thing as substituting an injured player. He moved to the second row, with Jimmy Nelson of Malone switching to number eight. But Ireland won 5–0, thanks to a McCarthy try. It was 364 days after JC Daly's historic try at Ravenhill and, once again, Ireland's breakthrough came early in the second half as a result of pressurising poor Frank Trott, the Welsh full-back. 'I can remember it clearly,' said McCarthy. 'There was a line-out on the left-hand side in front of the stand, and Ernie Strathdee passed it to Jack, running left, only a few yards in from the touchline. Something told me he's going to have to cross kick this so I took off towards the posts. I arrived on Frank Trott's chest just as the ball was coming down and it stuck in my mitts. And no, I wasn't off-side. I was never offside in my life ...'

Photographs from St Helen's show fairly subdued post-match scenes. No pitch invasion – even the folks crammed into the balconies high above the ground held their positions. At least on this occasion, someone had arranged a post-match party. That someone, it seems, was IRFU President Sarsfield Hogan, who put on a few drinks for the winning team. 'The hotel in Porthcawl was stocked up with free booze for the team – and you never got anything free in those days,' said O'Brien. 'It was a long night as I recall – there were only about three of us who drank.' Innocent times.

1982

For the vast majority of us, the teams of the late 1940s only ever existed in a black-and-white world. By 1982, the majority of Irish homes had a colour television but that didn't stop Ireland from being a colourless and often depressing place. There were IRA hunger strikes in the Maze Prison and the Attorney General was harbouring a murderer by the name of McArthur. This was six years before Stuttgart, where Ray Houghton put the ball in the England net, eight years before a famous penalty shoot-out in Genoa. We didn't yet know that sport could have a mood-altering effect on an entire nation.

Looking across a 33-year gap, it's easy to see certain parallels. For Jack Kyle, read Ollie Campbell; for McKay–McCarthy–O'Brien, read Slattery–Duggan–O'Driscoll; and for Karl Mullen, the relatively inexperienced hooker who was unexpectedly tossed the captaincy, read newly appointed Ciaran Fitzgerald. At the time, all you could see was a lousy run of defeats and an ageing pack of forwards. The press dubbed them 'Dad's Army'. It wasn't meant as a term of endearment.

Ireland went into the 1982 campaign having lost seven of their previous eight games and having drawn the other – and that was against Romania. They were all narrow losses, which made it all the more frustrating for Fitzgerald, who missed the season through injury. 'I couldn't believe we were being beaten. There was almost the entire pack of forwards from the tour to Australia in 1979 where we'd won both tests. They were totally dominant but we were losing games through silly mistakes. So there was a bit of pressure on when it came to the final trial in January. I was delighted when I saw they'd made me captain of the "possibles" because they'd put all the old fellas in that side. It was a warning to all of them that, to stay in, they had to produce. I knew they weren't going to cry off the trial, as established players often did.

'There was a hunger there to restore a bit of credibility. They were fed up to the gills being told they were wankers by everyone in the country. They all had their own agendas. They'd all played with guys from other countries away with the Lions. They never wanted to be remembered for the way the 1981 season went. They got fit, too. Mossie Keane used to live down the road from me and I used to train with him on a Monday and a Wednesday night, which was unheard of for Mossie. It was the same with Willie Duggan. There are lots of stories about Willie and the cigarettes, but Willie trained in his own way and was fitter than people realised. For these guys, being put into the Blues (or possibles) for the final trial was rubbing their nose in it a bit.'

The old lags duly delivered and were given another chance. As for Campbell, the selectors took a leap of faith. They had tried to accommodate

Phil Orr (centre) and Willie Duggan (right), two soldiers from the 'Dad's Army' pack
of 1982, follow the flight of an Ollie Campbell line-kick.

both him and Tony Ward in the team the previous season, with Campbell
switching to centre. It hadn't worked. Now Campbell was short on match
practice, having taken a self-imposed three-month break from the game
before Christmas. But he felt sharp in the couple of club games he played
for Old Belvedere. Legend has it that Duggan and Fergus Slattery heaped
a pile of money on Ireland to win the championship once they heard
Campbell would be wearing the number ten shirt.

That Campbell had felt the need to take a break from the game says
something about his approach to rugby. He was a fanatical trainer and

hadn't taken a proper holiday from the game in seven years. If George Norton had been dedicated to kicking practice, Campbell was obsessive about it. 'I look back now and realise how ridiculous it was,' he recalled. 'In the mornings, it took two buses to get from Malahide to the College of Commerce in Rathmines. At lunchtime, I'd get the 18 bus from Rathmines to the top of Anglesea Road, do an hour's kicking and then get the bus back to college. I'd be back down to Belvo later on for training. I had to come to an understanding with the caretaker, Christy Kavanagh. He wasn't happy about it but finally he agreed to let me turn the floodlights off after I'd finished my kicking routine on the back pitch.'

You have to wonder how the IRFU viewed Campbell's quasi-professional approach. They certainly did little to encourage him in his quest for perfection. Fitzgerald tried on numerous occasions to get him a few new match balls but the union consistently fobbed him off. Even the idea of having squad sessions before the appointed assembly time – forty-eight hours before kickoff – was questioned. Training sessions were basic. It would invariably begin with a game of tip-rugby – married forwards against bachelor backs. Then the two units would go their separate ways and the forwards would work almost exclusively on the set pieces. They didn't see the team as entertainers, and there was no point in giving the ball to the three-quarters either.

For all that, there were three tries in the first game of the championship, a 20–12 win against the Welsh. All three were scored by wingers too, with one sublime sequence of dummy-sidestep-dummy-pass by Campbell to set up the first of two by Moss Finn. Just a pity that afterwards Finn could recall nothing of his tries. Having been concussed earlier in the game, the first he knew of them was from watching *Rugby Special* in St Vincent's Hospital the following afternoon.

'The only thing we were thinking about going into the game was stopping the rot,' said Campbell. 'Beating the Welsh was still a big deal – we'd gone throughout the '70s without winning once. Afterwards, there was just this sense of belief. Certainly, there was no talk of a Triple Crown.'

That didn't come until after Twickenham and a win over a side that had won the Grand Slam two years previously. Bill Beaumont, their skipper, missed this game, however, and the Irish pack was rampant. It isn't necessary to recall the sequence leading to Ginger McLoughlin's try, seeing as half the Irish population claim to have been seated in that corner of the ground at the time. But the conversion, from the right touchline, across an impossible wind was surely Campbell's best strike of the championship.

'In terms of being through the eye of a needle, yes, sure,' he said. 'It also turned out to be important in that we ended up winning by a point: 16–15. But what stayed with me afterwards was a missed kick in the first half, 35 yards out, just to the left of the post. I started it off left to allow for the breeze and it held its line. It was so irritating that on the Sunday I went straight from Dublin Airport to Old Belvedere and did an hour's kicking, all from the same spot. Eventually I had to be moved along. The seconds were playing against Drogheda.'

Elsewhere, the hype was building. Fitzgerald remembers a crowded, chaotic training session the Sunday before the Scotland game at the Wanderers Club on Merrion Road. 'You have to remember there were no world cups back then, no Heineken cups. The Triple Crown was huge, bigger than winning the championship. I wasn't training because I'd a septic thumb but I was there in my civvies trying to organise line-outs. I was like a clown. It was an absolutely useless session, the crowd talking to the players and everything. You were just longing for Thursday, to get into the Shelbourne Hotel and close the door.'

This provided only limited insulation. By match day, the hotel was mobbed and Campbell can still recall the swell of voices as the players emerged into the foyer. 'Then suddenly you're out there on the pitch and, three minutes in, Clive Norling awards us a penalty and it's from that same spot – 35 metres out, slightly left of the posts, downwind. Of the hundreds of kicks I'd taken in the previous fortnight, 90 percent were from that very spot. It sounds easy to say now, but I could have kicked it with my eyes shut.' He would kick another five and throw in a drop-goal to finish with

Ciaran Fitzgerald and Moss Finn are cheered off the Lansdowne Road pitch after beating Scotland 21–12 in 1982 – the first Triple Crown in 33 years. Now for a Grand Slam? No, the Slam could wait.

twenty-one points, a championship record. It was a drab game but Campbell could sense the crowd in the old East Stand standing and singing for the entire second half, or so it seemed at the time.

His scrapbook shows the clippings – 'Ollie for Taoiseach' (it was election week) – and snaps of wild celebrations in O'Donoghue's of Merrion Row. The famously abstemious Campbell even had a pint or two that night. And as Fitzgerald said, it will always be remembered as Campbell's Triple Crown. 'Without a doubt. Everything revolved around him. He set up those tries and scored all those points but his contribution in defence was even more amazing. For such a slight fella, he was technically brilliant. He could tackle any forward and not get hurt himself because he could take them so low. It was only afterwards when you watched the videos that you realised the amount of work the guy used to do.'

For some, the party went on for a month. Ireland went to Paris, supposedly in search of a Grand Slam but were blown away. Campbell kicked three penalties to bring his championship tally to 46, equalling the record he had set two years earlier. But he was devastated. 'It was a shame, because you don't get opportunities like that often,' he said. 'Still, late on that night, I remember a supporter, Jimmy Smyth from Blackrock, coming up to me outside the Hotel Concorde St Lazare, telling me not to worry, they hadn't come to see Ireland winning a Grand Slam, they'd come to celebrate a Triple Crown. He had a few on him, but it put things in perspective.'

1985

Two years later, Campbell's career was over because of chronic hamstring problems. As for Fitzgerald, he had fallen from quite a height. While Ireland could 'only' manage a share of the championship title in 1983, the skipper was rewarded for his efforts with the captaincy of the Lions side to tour New Zealand that summer. That was when his troubles began. The British press hammered on about how England's Peter Wheeler and Scotland's Colin Deans were better hookers than Fitzgerald, with the captain's line-out throwing coming in for some relentless criticism. It only intensified when the Lions lost the test series 4–0.

Hugo MacNeill, the Lions' full-back for the first two tests, reckons Fitzgerald wasn't helped by having an over-protective manager in Willie John McBride, who then took over as Ireland coach. Either way, the downward spiral continued in the next championship season, when Ireland were whitewashed. Disappointment turned to acrimony following the second game against Wales, during which Fitzgerald had to be substituted because of a cut over his eye. He was then 'left out' for the game against England, 'for his own safety', according to the selectors, even though he had been passed fit by the team's medical staff.

Harry Harbison took his place for the two remaining games, with Willie Duggan taking over as captain. At 32, Fitzgerald must have been tempted to jack it in.

Fitzgerald didn't consider the thought for long. 'There was an element of personal vindication, particularly after the Lions experience. Then I got dropped in '84 and there was the manner in which it happened. Either I was fit or I wasn't fit. I remember I went up to Dungannon and played with St Mary's on the day Ireland were playing England, just to make the point. I would have preferred to have been told straight up but I suppose Willie John did things his way. The following season, I just decided to have a good cut at it.'

There were other catalysts for Fitzgerald. McBride, the soft-spoken pipe-smoker, had been replaced by brash, bold Mick Doyle. There was a new cast of players too. The team that lost 9–16 to the grand-slamming Wallabies in November had five new caps – Michael Bradley, Brendan Mullin, Willie Anderson, Philip Matthews and Willie Sexton – while Nigel Carr and Brian Spillane would make their debuts in the championship opener in Edinburgh. There was also an approach to the game that was, frankly, distinctly un-Irish. The 67 points they would score in the championship were all scored by backs, and their five tries – two of them classics – were all scored by the three-quarters.

Doyle's catch-phrase of 'Give it a lash' now seems trite, but it was appropriate at the time. To some extent, it was a case of making it up as he went along. The coach might not, for example, have happened across Michael Kiernan as a record-breaking goal-kicker had Moss Finn not picked up a knock in the first half against Australia. The selectors also took a big gamble in pairing Bradley and Paul Dean at half-back – one a rookie, the other a converted centre. As Bradley recalls it, the first time they played together was in Musgrave Park early that season, in a fundraiser for Pat Carroll, a Sunday's Well member who had suffered a serious injury. Whether or not they realised it at the time, it was the beginning of something special.

'There's a simple reason why we ran the ball so much,' said Bradley, smiling. 'Paul Dean can't kick. He was a genius with ball in hand, however, creating space, putting people through gaps. Doyler recognised that and recognised the speed available to him on the outside – Michael Kiernan was a sprint champion, so was Brenny Mullin, while Keith Crossan was as fast. It just made sense.'

This side's approach to training was also different. Backs and forwards actually worked together – a revolutionary approach in the mid-80s. Doyle even threatened to get scientific, enlisting the advice of a dietician from the Blackrock Clinic, who planned to come up with personalised diets for the players. 'She was exactly what was needed but she was banished as soon as the Irish medical fraternity heard about it,' recalled Fitzgerald. 'The players were being advised to eat less red meat and some people didn't like this getting into the public domain.'

Having played full-back on the '82 side, MacNeill was as well placed as anyone to see the contrast in approach. 'There was a lot of confidence for a young side. A lot of guys had played together at schools level and for the universities, guys who were used to being winners – Matthews, Carr, Mannix [Donal Lenihan], Brads. We used to look forward to meeting up at the Shelbourne for training weekends. We'd have nights out together but then train fanatically hard the next day. I must have been a pain in the ass I was so fanatical and single-minded. I was the sort of guy who had gone back to Blackrock for an extra year to win a schools cup, and dropped guys off the side for the slightest faltering in commitment. But it wasn't just me. We were all incredibly competitive.'

And they had the perfect facilitator. A lot was written about Mick Doyle when he died in tragic circumstances shortly after the 2004 team had won the Triple Crown and, as happens when someone dies, the description of his contribution to society was perhaps overblown. Speaking before his death, his former charges spoke enthusiastically and honestly about the qualities Doyle brought. He may not have been a great technician or a meticulous planner. But he did inspire.

'You need someone to be the catalyst,' said MacNeill. 'You need someone to say, "You can actually do this." He caught the spirit of an already confident group, he lit the touchpaper. You couldn't say he coached the side in the strictest sense but he was very important in that liberating aspect. It was a bit like champagne in that it had fizzled out by the following season. But at the time he inspired us like no-one else probably could have done.'

Doyle had done so much talking about freedom and self-expression that there was an enormous sense of anti-climax when the first game of the championship – England at home – was cancelled because of snow. The pent-up energy made for an explosive start to the game against Scotland, the Grand Slam champions, in Edinburgh two weeks later. The first time Ireland got their hands on the ball, they spun it. Crazy stuff – Crossan popping up in midfield, Mullin gliding through a gap, MacNeill stopped in the left corner by Iwan Tukalo (MacNeill still curses himself for carrying the ball under his right arm). No score but an eloquent statement of intent.

In part, this bravado was fuelled by a determination to damn the begrudgers. For there were begrudgers, a sizeable contingent of them, who were appalled that Ireland could enter a Five Nations game without a recognised goal kicker, especially when Tony Ward was available. There must have been snorts of derision when Kiernan missed three kicks at goal in the first half, while Peter Dods was banging them over at the other end. Kiernan did drop a goal, however, and Ireland edged ahead just after the break, courtesy of an outrageous behind-the-back flick by Bradley to Ringland. However, it's Ringland's second try that is replayed more often, and it's the score that ultimately silenced the Tony Ward supporters club. Trailing 12–15 in injury time, this was the last throw of the dice. It was a team try but it was also all about Paul Dean – maybe only Mark Ella could have matched it – scooping Bradley's pass off his ankle, looping around Kiernan, dummying, straightening and then off-loading to Mullin in the tackle. MacNeill then made amends for his earlier gaffe with a deliciously floated scoring pass.

'I'll never forget the dressing room afterwards,' said MacNeill. 'No-one could sit down. I'd never been part of something in rugby as exhilarating.

You were thinking that all around Ireland, there were kids now going out in back gardens to relive that try.'

There was very little reliving of the 15–15 draw against France in Dublin four weeks later. The only benefit derived from a filthy game was that it served to unify what was still a largely untried side.

The defining image from Cardiff two weeks later is the Irish team linking arms for the singing of 'Land of My Fathers' before the game. The day before the game, Doyle denied that his team were under any more pressure than normal because Ireland hadn't won at the Arms Park since 1967: 'The lads don't give a f*** about what's happened to the Irish team in Cardiff for the past eighteen years,' he told reporters. 'They don't give a bugger about the reputation of the Arms Park, its history and all that stuff.' Fitzgerald now admits he was struck by the volume of noise within the old stadium – even when the players were strolling around the pitch in their blazers an hour before kickoff. Just one anthem would be played – the Welsh one. The

UNION · FAMOUS GROUSE SCOTCH WHISKY

linking of arms was a premeditated gesture of defiance, and defiance was written all over the faces of the players.

Well, most of them. Peter Thursfield's well-known photograph (above) shows that at the far end of the line from Fitzgerald, Spillane is bellowing out the song. This, remember, is a matter of minutes before he would play his second game for Ireland. Bradley, standing third from the right, was perplexed. 'The Welshmen are standing beside us and you had 60,000 Welshmen roaring and Spillane is singing his head off. I said, "What are you singing that for?" and he said, "I *love* this song." That's the kind of free spirit that was in that team. It was just a group of fellas who wanted to go out and play ball.'

Which is what this side did best. The set pieces were poor, with a line-out count of 19–7 in Wales's favour, yet Ireland still came away with a 21–9 win – Ireland's biggest ever win in Cardiff. One reason was the goal kicking. While Kiernan kicked every opportunity that came his way, the

Ciaran Fitzgerald. 'We'd prepared a call for those situations. It was like pressing a button, a turbo charge, if you like.'

normally dependable Welsh full-back Mark Wyatt kicked one from six – a performance that became legendary in its awfulness. The other reason was Ireland's finishing. Once again, Bradley and Ringland combined to squeeze a try from nothing in the first half. And once again, the match winner was the result of Dean's straight running and MacNeill's wonderfully timed intervention.

The script writers, who arranged for the opening game to be postponed, appeared to have got it right. After two great wins on the road in Edinburgh and Cardiff, Ireland had been provided with the perfect ending – a Triple Crown decider at home to England. 'The great thing about Ireland is the whole country goes on an adventure,' said MacNeill. 'It doesn't matter whether it's with Jack Charlton, Sonia O'Sullivan or Stephen Roche. There's none of the fashionable cynicism like you used to get in England. You've got to remember 1985 was a time of 20 percent unemployment, crucifying tax rates and mass emigration. It was before Bono or The Corrs, before the Irish developed this confidence abroad. I think we caught the imagination of the public because of the way we played. It was so free. It was youth gone mad, given its head. Whereas 1982 had been about pragmatism, now anything was possible.'

Except an Irish defeat. England, directed by a 22-year-old out-half by the name of Rob Andrew, weren't really given much of a chance, even though they were still in with a chance of a share of the championship. Heavy showers on the morning of the game weren't ideal but everything was still running to schedule when Mullin blocked Chris Martin's clearance to score midway through the first half. But it developed into an ugly, nervy mud-fest, one for which the heavier England pack was much better suited. Kiernan's place-kicking deteriorated as the game went on. Meanwhile, Rory Underwood's try meant the teams were tied at 10–10 with five minutes remaining when Andrew was presented with a penalty 40 metres out to the left of the Irish posts. It was well within his range. 'There was this awful moment when you're staring into the abyss,' says MacNeill. 'You're standing near the posts while Andrew has this kick and you're powerless to do anything about it. But he pulled it and so we had one last chance.'

This, by common consent, is the moment when millions of lip-readers around the world saw Fitzgerald ask the immortal question: 'Where's your f***ing pride?'

'We were starting to struggle badly so we needed something extra,' Fitzgerald recalled. 'We'd prepared a call for such situations. It was like pressing a button, a turbo charge, if you like. We used it against Scotland, for the try at the death. It was the same here. We used a short drop-out to Brian Spillane, one we'd practised all season but never used and that got us out of our half. Once we'd done that, I knew we had a chance.'

Watching reruns of the Kiernan drop-goal, a couple of things catch the

eye. First there is the fact that the English defenders were incredibly generous in the time and space they allowed him as the ball emerged from the
ruck. Second there is the manic reaction of the crowd at the Havelock
Square end. Also, if you ever wondered who Kiernan was wagging his
finger at as he ran back, it was Keith Crossan. About a minute earlier, Kiernan had told him he might chance a drop-goal. It was just as well Kiernan
was on target for there was a two-man overlap to his right.

There was no lap of honour at the final whistle, no choreographed celebrations. It was all about avoiding the crowd that flooded onto the pitch.
Fitzgerald just happened to be standing on the touchline under the West
Stand when Jim Fleming blew for full time, so he grabbed the match ball
and disappeared. Within minutes, he was prevailed upon to reappear for
the crowd. If he didn't, he was told, there was a danger the crowd would
come to him. 'So I went back out,' he said. 'I felt a bit funny, just standing
there on a seat in the stand for five or six minutes. I didn't know what I was
doing. It was just to react to the crowd.'

You can see why this essentially modest man would have felt uncomfortable. Unlike 1982, which will be remembered as Ollie Campbell's Triple
Crown, this had been a true team achievement, and for that reason it holds
happier memories for the skipper. But on another level, it was about
Fitzgerald's personal triumph, about banishing the demons that lingered
from the Lions tour two years earlier. He may have felt awkward, standing
there alone before the happy, heaving multitude. Yet, in a sense, it was the
perfect conclusion to a heart-warming tale.

CHAPTER 2 – FRANCE

DUCKS OUT OF LINE

The recurring image of Mick Doyle, and the one that accompanied most of the obituaries that were written about him, has a vast smile on those ruddy cheeks and a whistle hanging from a piece of hairy twine around his neck. Public perception of Eddie O'Sullivan is probably based primarily on those frantic flash interviews only minutes after the final whistle, when he delivers cold, analytical assessments whether Ireland have won or lost. Both men have coached successful Ireland teams but it's hard to think of two more contrasting personalities. Whereas one was the Corinthian who played wherever life took him, the other is the professional who lives for his work. While Doyle shot from the hip, O'Sullivan makes certain his target is in the cross hairs before squeezing the trigger. If the 'larger than life' cliché was applied to Doyle, O'Sullivan is the most self-contained of public figures.

Once O'Sullivan had emulated his predecessor in winning a Triple Crown, it was inevitable that his public profile would grow, whether he wanted it to or not. A few weeks after the victory over Scotland, viewers of *The Late, Late Show* got a more sympathetic view of the man originally from Youghal, County Cork, now resident in Moylough, County Galway, husband to Noreen, dad to Katie and Barry. We got Eddie in an open-neck shirt, all anecdotes and smiles. We got to hear about his fascination for explorers and exploration, for Shackleton, Crean and Cooke. We heard about his time spent spreading the rugby gospel with George Hook in the United States. A few weeks after that, O'Sullivan agreed to take part in a new RTÉ series, *Buried Alive*, where, with a studio audience, he watched video footage of various friends and colleagues commenting on him, as if he were already dead – a sort of 'This Was Your Life'.

It's unthinkable that O'Sullivan was on the lookout for extra exposure. He is a consummate media pro, someone who puts thought into his press conferences and – Hallelujah! – someone who can make public utterances in complete, articulate sentences. Lazy questions may get curt responses and the odd withering stare, but O'Sullivan will fill up your notebook and it's usually quality stuff. He doesn't crave the microphones or cameras, however. As with everything else, it's just part of the job. If he had the choice, he'd rather not – thanks all the same.

He has an aversion to crowds. Before becoming Ireland coach, he had only been to Lansdowne Road once as a spectator. He likes music but doesn't like concerts. His hobbies – reading, watching television, doing the *Irish Times* Simplex crossword – are all solitary activities. While he is an excellent communicator of ideas and stratagems, he is essentially introverted. As he said shortly after taking over as Ireland coach, 'Tell me you don't like me and I don't really care. If you said you didn't respect me, then I'd be upset.'

The players *do* respect their coach. 'Technically, he's outstanding,' said Ronan O'Gara. 'And I'm in a position where I appreciate it. An awful lot of my work is done on the training pitch and I benefit from what Eddie brings to it in terms of the preparatory stuff. If the patterns fall into shape during the week, then I've a lot less to worry about come game time. There are a number of game plans, depending on a number of factors – it's very detailed stuff, very fine-tuned. You could be discussing what you'll do, say, off scrums in a certain area of the pitch, thinking maybe four phases ahead. I suppose the more senior I've got, the more advanced our relationship has become in terms of talking strategies. I kind of feel comfortable talking to him and if I'm not happy with something, then I say no. Maybe I didn't in the past and that was my own fault. Now I think everything can be discussed.'

It would be stretching things to characterise Ireland's coach as a dictator. There are times when the coach will canvass the opinions of his senior

Figuring out the angle. Former maths teacher Eddie O'Sullivan considers another media question during the build-up to the French match in Paris.

players before coming to a decision. Yet you won't see him socialising with his players on the night after a test match, as Warren Gatland, his predecessor as Ireland coach, used to do. Once the obligatory flesh-pressing has been done, he could well be up in his hotel room, poring over the match video.

'Eddie's very methodical,' said Paul O'Connell. 'Half of the stuff he does, you don't see it happening. You just know you're due at a certain place at a certain time and you're there for a very specific reason. In fairness to him, none of the problems seep down to the players, which is brilliant. You know what you're doing and by and large it's the right thing to do and there's no debate about it. He is a bit cold, I suppose, but he has to be like that. It's hard to be friends with guys when you're chopping and changing, bawling people out of it on the pitch, which is happening a lot now. We're becoming more critical of each other on the training pitch and in the video sessions, which is the way it should be. In that context, I suppose it's hard to be buddy-buddy with your players.'

'Players like structure, they like discipline and that's what the get from Eddie,' said John Redmond, nominally the team's press officer but also part-minder to whoever needs minding, part-bouncer and part-security officer. 'Essentially, they like to know what they're doing next. All this is worked out well in advance. Every morning we're in camp, the management team has a working breakfast meeting, usually at 8.30, sometimes earlier. Everyone has to outline their plans for the day. Eddie's trademark is thoroughness, organisation, never leaving anything to chance.'

You could say he has a phobia about disorganisation. In O'Sullivan-speak, that distinctive idiom developed during his time in the US, there are a few descriptions for the state of being in which things are not as they should be. It's a 'Keystone Cops scenario', or 'everybody's running around with their hair on fire'. When this happens, then 'your ass (or your *cojones*) is in the bacon slicer' and this same ass (or *cojones*) is 'about to be served up to you on a plate'. Essentially, O'Sullivan craves the happiness of knowing that his 'ducks are in a row'.

As the 2004 Six Nations approached, it looked, to those of us on the periphery, like the coach's ducks were anything but. There was a staleness in the air after the Rugby World Cup, and a general dissatisfaction with Ireland's performance in Australia. Almost all of the credit earned by out-playing the host nation (to lose by a point) had been erased by a jaded-looking non-performance in the quarter-final against France, who won 43–21. Afterwards, O'Sullivan did himself few favours by claiming that his team had had a 'very, very good tournament'. While there was a difference of opinion as to the number of verys employed, there was unanimity on one thing – a suggestion of spin had been applied to that cold, rational post-game analysis.

Then a few hairline cracks started to appear in the support structure the coach had built beneath him. Eight days after defeat to France, a story appeared in the *Belfast Telegraph* in which Mike McGurn, the team's fitness coach, made a few incendiary comments about the training structures the IRFU had put in place. This, McGurn claimed, was the main reason for that poor performance against France.

'We need a fitness revolution in Irish rugby,' McGurn told Gavin Mairs. 'Previously we have had to work under the realms of the provinces and then myself. But the way forward for Eddie and myself is to have total autonomy of the national players. That means I will be controlling all aspects of fitness and strength for the next four years. Some of our players are only operating on 60 to 70 percent of their capacity, and that includes Brian O'Driscoll, because of the lack of a pre-season [fitness programme] and too many games over the course of a season. The quarter-final was a game too far for us. A lack of pre-season only allows you to have so many big games in the tank. We had big games against Argentina and Australia, but the French game was a game too far. Our pack was tired, our backs looked slow. They were much more powerful and much quicker than us. I can get players fit, fast and strong but I don't need roadblocks in my way when I am trying to do that.'

McGurn's comments caused quite a stir. Not only had he demeaned the provincial fitness coaches, he had criticised his boss, Dr Liam Hennessy, the IRFU's national director of fitness and, by extension, the union itself. Senior figures in Lansdowne Road were furious at this public outburst and McGurn was summoned home from Australia, where he was on holiday, to explain himself. It was widely predicted that he would lose his job, but it was a complicated situation – McGurn was claiming he had already been offered a four-year extension to his IRFU contract. Whatever the intricacies of the legal battle that followed, O'Sullivan would find himself minus a fitness coach, with Hennessy stepping in for the time being.

He was minus a scrum-coach too – Tony D'Arcy, the Australian who had been part of the coaching team, was informed after the World Cup that his services were no longer required. And all along, there was the thorny issue of O'Sullivan's relationship with his assistant coach, Declan Kidney. Kidney had been foisted on O'Sullivan in the first place, which was one of the union's less enlightened moves. A head honcho by inclination, Kidney was never going to be happy in an auxiliary role. Now O'Sullivan's contract had been extended until 2008 and he had been given the right to hire and fire his staff. When it emerged in February that the union had offered Kidney a desk job, it was clear that O'Sullivan had pressed the release button. Yet because Kidney was contracted as assistant coach until July, this already fraught relationship would continue for the duration of the championship. Hardly ideal.

O'Sullivan hadn't been winning any popularity contests in the provinces either. The World Cup had meant the top players had barely made an appearance before late November, with Leinster and Munster operating on skeleton staffs in the Celtic League. They were welcomed back with open arms for the first two rounds of Heineken Cup action but the reunion was short-lived. The Sunday after the second round of Heineken matches, the players were off again, this time for a week's fitness camp in Lanzarote. This had always been scheduled, but the arrangement at short notice of another mini-camp in January caused barely suppressed fury in Thomond Park and Donnybrook. 'The timing of that camp was an absolute disaster for us,' said Gary Ella, the Leinster coach, at the end of the season. 'You shouldn't have guys coming back from the World Cup, playing a couple of Heineken Cup games and then having to go off to an Irish camp. We then had people carrying injuries into the next Heineken Cup week. It was ridiculous.' It's unlikely O'Sullivan got a Christmas card from the Ulster Branch either – for a while, there were fears David Humphreys wouldn't be released for Ulster's Celtic Cup final against Edinburgh in Murrayfield.

O'Sullivan defended his plans stoutly. 'It's a nonsense to be giving out about Lanzarote. It's in the calendar every year,' he said. 'I know the provincial directors want the players as much as possible but I'm working off a 15-test schedule this year following on from 14 tests last season. Twenty-nine tests in two seasons; that's unprecedented in Irish rugby. There is a tension there and it's not anybody's fault. It's just the way the season is.

There was a fatigue factor after the World Cup so bringing them to Spain for that break was very important. The players got a huge benefit from it, so it was actually of benefit to the provinces as well.'

It should be said that the players enjoy the Lanzarote trips, although those with wives and children probably have some explaining to do. The fitness work has a refreshing effect and they like being able to take a dip in the Atlantic after training when everyone at home is in December mode. This year, however, the news that filtered back made it look a bit like the players were enjoying themselves too much.

On the final night, the team management ran a tab behind the hotel bar so that the players could have a few Christmas drinks. This didn't prevent training the next morning, of course, and when roommates Malcolm O'Kelly and Anthony Horgan failed to turn up on time, O'Sullivan came down heavily on them. Not only were they suspended from the mini-camp in Dublin in early January, the suspension would be made public. It was better, he explained to the players, to be up-front than to have the news leak out, as would inevitably happen. Besides, it was a serious issue. As O'Sullivan said: 'It was too serious an incident to handle internally. They didn't show up for training, something I wasn't happy about. It didn't give me any great pleasure but at the same time I had to face up to it. If I didn't, I'd have been giving out the wrong message. It was a bit of a story for a couple of days because it hadn't happened before. It wasn't an overreaction or an underreaction. They were told they were out. The one thing they were told was that was their punishment. It wouldn't be held against them.

'To be honest, I don't think things were at all as gloomy as people thought. There was the Mike McGurn situation when he went out on a limb and made some statements he shouldn't have made, personal opinions that basically criticised the union. It wasn't the ideal thing. But, like every problem, you deal with it. It wasn't that difficult to deal with because we weren't actually in camp at the time. I stepped away from it because it was a employer/employee issue, as far as I was concerned. It wasn't as big a deal as people made it out to be. I wasn't unduly worried. There were a few problems which came down the pike that I could have done without. But I didn't see any long-term fallout.'

This was spoken with the benefit of hindsight. At the time, there were mutterings of discontent within the squad. Why, some players wondered, had O'Sullivan apparently done nothing to support McGurn, who was so popular and highly rated amongst the players? There were some who felt the treatment of O'Kelly and Horgan had been heavy-handed. 'It was a bit harsh,' said one player. 'There could have been some means of keeping it in-house. It would have been dealt with differently at provincial level.'

On his appointment two years previously, O'Sullivan made it clear he believed having a team of specialist coaches was the way forward. Now, that team was beginning to dwindle: McGurn was out of the picture, D'Arcy had been dismissed and Kidney was soon to follow. The post-World Cup vacuum left plenty of room for speculation. Was O'Sullivan beginning to look a little isolated? Was he already missing the recently retired Keith Wood, who had been his friend as well as his true second-in-command?

To complicate matters further, Brian O'Driscoll, Wood's heir apparent, was having problems of his own (that would have been 'Hair Apparent', in the tabloids, of course). The media, let it be said, were on O'Driscoll's case. He was getting stick for earning too much money. He was getting stick for plugging his sponsors too obviously in interviews. He was getting stick for supposedly being overweight – despite the fact that *Social & Personal* magazine named him as 'Ireland's Sexiest Man'. He was getting stick for a dodgy new hairstyle, which, it was suggested, was a by-product of his long-term relationship with a fashion model. The Posh 'n' Becks analogies were just too tempting to ignore.

The captain had O'Sullivan's sympathy. 'I think we have a paradigm shift for rugby players that we're only just beginning to realise. They're not just rugby players, they're also celebrities. As Irish pro sportsmen go, Brian mightn't earn as much as Pádraig Harrington but he's every bit as recognisable. Everywhere he goes in Ireland, he's recognised. He's on billboards, he's on TV ads. He's twenty-five years of age, he's the sexiest man in

The life of Brian. The Ireland captain sits through another inquisition by the media, probably hoping there won't be any more questions about his hair.

Ireland, kinda thing. So, what now happens is that he attracts attention from people in the media who wouldn't normally have an interest in rugby players. They'd normally be more interested in a juicy story on a soccer player. They suddenly realise they have a new target. He appears in some social columns and he's got a high-profile girlfriend. He is a superstar of Irish sport. And that attention is all new. I don't think he's ever said, "I'm over here, come here and take pictures of me." The good thing is he's smart enough to know there's no point in fighting or worrying about something you can't control.'

Having monitored O'Driscoll since his international debut as a 20-year-old, team press officer John Redmond has seen media attitudes towards him oscillate between adulation, vilification and good old-fashioned invasion of privacy. 'Brian's arrival has coincided with an improvement in the fortunes of the Irish rugby team but it has also coincided with a huge shift in media attitudes. There's the shift towards the cult of the personality but unfortunately there's also the vanishing gulf between the established quality journalism and tabloid. There used to be a huge difference but now, because of commercialisation, it's wafer thin. We now live with news television stations, commercial radio stations, more and more newspaper titles and websites. There's so much news that every item has to be different. We're constantly moving the fine line between what will sell and what won't.

'We've never really had a player who transcends his sport before and this is the world he walks into. It means he can't walk into a bar and order a drink without a photographer taking a picture and looking to sell it. It also means that if he doesn't score a try, this translates into him having a bad game. It's the Posh and Becks things. We crave figures like that and yet we resent figures like that. And if we see anyone getting close to that, we move in.'

Sure enough, the *Evening Herald* moved in with a flimsy front-page story about O'Driscoll and his girlfriend being spotted in Renard's, a Dublin nightclub. The 'story' was based on unattributed quotes from 'senior figures from within rugby HQ' who thought that O'Driscoll's lifestyle was 'more in line with a pop star than an athlete'. There was, supposedly, '... some annoyance that Brian is being increasingly seen as a celebrity rather than a rugby player. The Posh and Becks talk and the peroxide hair do not go down well with the powers that be.'

Speaking a few months later, on the eve of Ireland's summer tour to South Africa, O'Driscoll was still touchy on the subject of this 'revelation'. 'There's a lot of fabrication out there,' he said. 'I understand that people have to sell newspapers so they'll present things as the truth or bend it as far as they want. Sometimes they'll just pick things from thin air and that was another one of those cases. I don't really care what people think or say about me, to be honest.'

At the time, though, he clearly did care. 'It has got to the point where it is something I have to deal with,' he told the *Daily Mail* in February. 'You can't let people walk all over you. You have to say when something is not true. I have never gone out less in my life since New Year's Eve. I do not live like a celebrity. What I hate about the invasion of my privacy is that I always have to watch what I am doing. I may be at a club with my friends drinking Coke. When I come outside I have to avoid having a joke or a laugh in case I am pictured falling about and people get the wrong idea. I can't go to certain places at certain times. I find that difficult to live with. I don't like having to look over my shoulder all the time. If you have two beers, you are on the lash. Worse than that, if you are seen out, you are on the lash. It is not ideal. I get invited to things which are fun. I want to live my life. I'm twenty-five, not eighty-five. Rugby is not the be-all and end-all. I am determined to make it a lot harder for people to write anything. I am not going to give them an easy life – and I am not going to be driven out of Ireland.'

This wasn't to say he wouldn't leave of his own volition, however. This was the message he put out as a guest on RTÉ's *Late, Late Show* a few weeks earlier. The viewers of Ireland's most-watched television programme learned that the best rugby player in the country – whose IRFU contract was then up for renegotiation – was considering a move abroad in search of silverware. It wasn't a move designed to please the folks at Lansdowne Road, or his Leinster team-mates, who just happened to be in France that weekend struggling for a slot in the quarter-finals of the Heineken Cup. O'Sullivan's number one duck, it seemed, was stepping out of line.

At this stage, however, the coach wasn't too concerned about what O'Driscoll said to Pat Kenny about his hair, his girlfriend or whatever. The most pressing issue was that his captain would almost definitely miss the championship opener in Paris. Friday, 9 January had been a bad night for Leinster and O'Sullivan. Not only had O'Driscoll ripped a hamstring, but Gary Ella's side, who had won their first two pool games, lost to Sale at Lansdowne Road. Their season never recovered. While Ella paid the ultimate price by losing his job, Leinster supporters pointed the finger at

O'Sullivan, who in their eyes had been hogging the top players. Their argument was strengthened the next day when Munster were blown off the pitch by Gloucester at Kingsholm.

There were just five weeks to go before Ireland played France in Paris on 14 February and newspaper subeditors were pencilling in the 'St Valentine's Day Massacre' headlines. More in hope than expectation, O'Sullivan named O'Driscoll captain for the Six Nations but also covered himself by naming five vice-captains – Anthony Foley, David Humphreys, Ronan O'Gara, Reggie Corrigan and Paul O'Connell. In reality, there was nothing new in this. When O'Driscoll had been appointed captain in Wood's absence the previous season, the same lieutenants had all been appointed to aid the new skipper in the decision-making process. All except O'Connell, that is. Everyone assumed his promotion was merely an acknowledgement of the impact he had had at the World Cup, when he had established himself as one of the world's best locks.

So it came as a shock to just about everyone when, on the Tuesday before the game in Paris, with O'Driscoll still out, 24-year-old Paul O'Connell had the asterisk beside his name on the team-sheet for Paris. The player had known for a couple of days at that stage but he admits he was taken by surprise when O'Sullivan first ran the idea past him. In fact, his first instinct told him he was in trouble. 'I hadn't an inkling. I thought it was brilliant to be made vice-captain. That was a big step for me. I didn't have a clue what Eddie had in mind. Even when I was asked up to his room, I thought it was because I was messing in training with Donncha. I thought I'd be pulled aside and told to cop on, that I was a vice-captain now. Donncha might have been on one team and me on the other and we might have been clipping each other in training. That's what I thought it was over.

'I was there, thinking, "What the f*** am I after doing?" Anthony Horgan said it first. "He's probably going to offer you the captaincy," he said jokingly, like, taking the piss out of me. He never thought it would happen either. But when I went up, Eddie asked me: "If Drico's out, do you want to captain the side?" I said I'd need a lot of help from the senior players, but I'd

Paul O'Connell listens intently during training. When Eddie O'Sullivan asked him to come to his room, O'Connell initially feared he was in for a lecture.

love to. I said if and when Drico was ruled out, maybe then he'd come back to me then and we'd have chat. He told me to tell no-one. Then he came back when it was definite and I'd no hesitation. We shook hands on it.

'It was cool. I suppose I'd gone OK in the tour to Tonga and Samoa the previous summer, when it was really shitty down there. From the sleeping conditions to the pitches, everything was shit down there. Tonga was bad. But a lot of us had gone well down there and got stuck into it. Then the World Cup went well for me, so … Anyway, when I told Hoggy, he was laughing his head off. That's how left-field it was.'

O'Sullivan denies that choosing O'Connell to lead the side was born of the need to invigorate a weary bunch of players. 'No, it's just that Paul is a warrior,' O'Sullivan said. 'I have a huge respect for guys who are warriors, who take the pressure, take the heat and still deliver. He's a go-to guy. He's prepared to talk for a start, he's prepared to take responsibility and he has the respect of the players. You can get plenty of guys who will talk, but people don't necessarily listen to them. You can get other people who'd be worth listening to, but don't talk. O'Connell is the kind of guy who does talk and people do listen to him.'

Having taken a punt on a new captain, it was time to pick a team. Those of us paid to scribble on such matters took a deep breath and were determined to be positive. It wasn't easy. If you looked at the pack of forwards that had started the previous game – against France, remember – half of them were playing for a thoroughly dispirited and lacklustre Leinster team that had just been walloped by a Biarritz team. Corrigan was struggling to shake off leg injuries and the credible replacements were thin on the ground. Malcolm O'Kelly looked like he was going through one of his distracted phases. As for Shane Byrne, the man scripted to take over from Keith Wood, there were those who believed Frankie Sheahan was a better bet. Interestingly, Wood was one of them.

There was also still uncertainty over who would start at out-half – Ronan O'Gara or David Humphreys – and no matter how O'Sullivan had tried to dress this up for the previous couple of years, to be fiddling around with the play-making role didn't instil confidence. As for the outside backs, things were a mess. The team's three best attackers – O'Driscoll, Geordan Murphy and Denis Hickie – were all missing through injury. And then you had Girvan Dempsey.

Poor Dempsey had a shocker almost every time he took to the rugby field. It wasn't easy to watch and it wasn't easy to write, because Dempsey is one of those model professionals and a thorough gentleman. Most successful pro sportspeople have a ruthless streak, a blinkered approach that shuts out doubt. Of all people, the international rugby full-back needs supreme self-belief. Dempsey's self-belief seemed to have evaporated. He had never been the most dynamic attacker and had always lacked evasion skills but the least you could expect was that he would catch, kick and tackle. Now, Leinster supporters were cringing whenever the ball was hoisted in his general direction. And if Dempsey did catch, he'd invariably slice the kick.

Almost as one, the rugby press decided that Dempsey should be dropped. If only for his own safety, he should be protected from the bombardment that would inevitably come out of the Paris sky. Think of the merciless shelling of John Kelly in Melbourne, we wrote. It would be verging on unkindness for O'Sullivan to pick Dempsey. Pick Gordon D'Arcy, in sensational form for Leinster, albeit in an unaccustomed role at outside centre. Pick Harlequins' Gavin Duffy, suggested someone else, even though this would mean blooding a 22-year-old full-back in Paris. 'Pick anyone,' said John O'Shea, an occasional rugby commentator, on TV3. 'Even Geordan Murphy on one leg is better than Dempsey.' Cruel stuff.

In the end, O'Sullivan stuck by him. He didn't really have an option – D'Arcy wasn't available for the full-back role because he was needed elsewhere, in O'Driscoll's outside centre slot. This was one of three changes from Melbourne. Tyrone Howe came in for Kelly on the left wing, while Anthony Foley reclaimed the number eight shirt from Victor Costello. Costello also lost out to Simon Easterby at number six, while Malcolm O'Kelly and Byrne just held off the challenges of Donncha O'Callaghan and Frankie Sheahan.

No-one, but no-one, predicted an Irish win. *L'Equipe* predicted it would be *'tout bleu, tout flamme'* – it would be all blue and the French would be on fire. The main purpose of the exercise, evidently, was to banish the painful memories of that World Cup semi-final hiding by England. And France's opponents? They were referred to *'Les Irlandais Orphelins'* – the Irish orphans – who were missing their 'parents' Wood and O'Driscoll.

The Irish press weren't really any more optimistic. It was noted that the French were poor starters, and that they would miss the highly influential Fabien Galthie, who had retired. But damage limitation was the all-pervasive theme – to avoid a repeat of Melbourne. A half-decent performance would improve the chances of winning what was perceived as the pivotal game of Ireland's championship – against Wales, eight days later. In many respects, Wales were the biggest threat of all. As the third game was against England at Twickenham, the possibility of having *nul points* after three games was all too real.

At least it seemed real to those of us on the outside looking in. We remember all too well what it was like in the 1990s. We are still conditioned to expect disappointment. We forget that the likes of Paul O'Connell loses less than 10 percent of the games he plays. He is conditioned to succeed.

Which is why he was still hurting a bit when Ireland travelled to Paris. The capitulation in that Melbourne quarter-final was anathema to O'Connell.

'It was such a major anti-climax,' he said. 'It had been a very good World Cup for me, and for a lot of us. I still don't know what happened that day. We're trying to cut out days like that, days that are reminiscent of the mid-90s or whenever. Still, the odd time they come back and haunt us. We were devastated but if you stayed like that for long, it was only going to affect your form in the European Cup and you couldn't let that happen, not with Munster anyway. I know people were saying there was a chance we might lose our first three matches and when you looked at it, you thought: Jesus, you may have a point there. It was a tough schedule with France and England away. But there's a lot of confidence there. We believed in the team, Eddie and Drico believed in the team. When you look at the amount of time we'd spent together before and during the World Cup, you'd think we'd go a bit stale but it wasn't like that at all. I suppose me having the captaincy for the first game was something different, something that people weren't used to. Then there was the fact that D'Arcy was in and playing so well. There were a few little changes which you need all the time to keep spicing it up.'

The squad and management team flew to Paris on Wednesday and then transferred to Versailles, where they were based until match day. Preparation didn't go absolutely to plan. Returning from training at the D'Orsay club on Friday, a strong smell of burning rubber caused a sudden, nervy evacuation of the team bus, after which the players were left sitting on the side of the street for half an hour. 'I don't want to sound melodramatic,' said John Redmond, 'but briefly there was a real sense of panic, the fear of an explosion with 40 people stuck beside a bus in this tiny village. It was something that you didn't want.'

Things did, however, go pretty much to plan for much of the first 40 minutes at the Stade de France, so much so that the stadium was practically asleep by half-time. By and large, it's an uninspiring place – a marvel of post-modern architecture to be sure, yet strangely soulless. Maybe it's because it's plonked in the outskirts, up in the concrete jungle of St Denis. Maybe it's because the spectators are so far from the action, separated as they are by a running track. Whatever it is, there are times when the Stade snoozes. (No bad thing, you may say. It's a blessing the French don't play all their home games in the cauldron that is the Velodrome of Marseilles.)

This was one of those times. It should be said that Ireland were largely responsible for the general drowsiness, sedating the French with their safety-first approach. O'Gara stood deep to avoid the marauding Serge Betsen and kicked the ball in behind the French back three. O'Connell called just about every ball on himself at the front of the line-out: safe, conservative, lacking ambition – but effective enough in that context.

With O'Gara kicking an early penalty, Ireland continued to play the territorial game and the latent French threat remained just that – latent. It wasn't until the twentieth minute that they drew level through a Frederic Michalak penalty. Shortly afterwards, they obliterated the Irish scrum to set up a try for Vincent Clerc and just briefly, the Stade was buzzing. It was a false alarm, however. At half time, by which stage Michalak had added another penalty, the game was back in safe mode.

The French needed a jab and they got it almost immediately after the restart. A lucky deflection and a neat chip and chase by O'Gara led to a try for Anthony Foley and O'Gara's conversion meant Ireland were trailing by a point at 11–10. Was this altogether wise? Within 10 minutes, France were ahead 25–10. A couple of defensive blunders allowed Pascal Papé and Yannick Jauzion to score sweet tries within four minutes of each other – that's 14 points in four minutes. There were all of 25 minutes remaining. Irish supporters braced themselves for a hammering.

It never happened. As the French sat back to admire their handiwork, Ireland began the slog again. It was deliberate, determined stuff compared to those few minutes of French elegance but it was admirable in its own way. There was one special moment, and it was provided by D'Arcy – a slashing half-break and daring off-load to Howe, who slid over near the right corner. France soon responded with a try by Jean-Baptiste Elissalde but, to their credit, Ireland were back on the front foot again when referee Chris White finally called time – France 35 Ireland 17.

The experience left you feeling a bit cold. It was reassuring that there had been no repeat of Melbourne, when Ireland had been slaughtered mercilessly for the first 50 minutes – here, the job was effectively done in a five-minute spell in the second half. But there was a sense of *ennui* about the French play after that, so it was hard to gauge the real value of Ireland's rearguard.

There were several encouraging individual performances. O'Gara had played with cool assurance and, notably, had been allowed to close the game out for once – previously, there had been every chance of a final-quarter substitution at out-half. Simon Easterby had vindicated his selection with a busy display, while Gordon D'Arcy had grown visibly in confidence as the game wore on. And no, Girvan Dempsey didn't have the shocker everyone predicted. But the collective philosophy drew a scathing response from some commentators. Brendan Fanning wrote the following in *The Sunday Independent*: 'In the old days Ireland came over here and gave thanks for each minute that passed without a score conceded. Yesterday they came with murder on their minds yet without malice: kill the game; deaden the crowd; and see what shape they were in after that. It's no way to play … We got the conservative guide to survival in France. Decent attacking positions were passed up by throwing the ball consistently to O'Connell at two in the lineout. The light was fading by the time they went wild and found Anthony Foley a bit further back. You wonder what France made of a team that got into the scoring zone and then took their foot off the pedal. As an exercise in inducing complacency in the opposition it was first class. But there was nothing false about France's sense of security … There were no smiles in the Irish bus as it pulled away

Tyrone Howe scores at the Stade de France. Very few people took too much comfort from Ireland's final-quarter fightback in Paris – except the management and players themselves.

from Stade de France. They got pretty much what they deserved.'

This – surprise, surprise – contrasted considerably with the message coming from Ireland's post-match press conference, where the focus was on what might have been but for that 14-point blast. Then again, what do we expect? It doesn't pay to dwell on negatives when you've got another test match in eight days' time.

'Whenever France were really tested, they pulled away from us quite comfortably and that's the sign of a good team,' said O'Gara. 'That said, I don't agree we went there negatively. It was about being practical. We knew how impressive their defence was, and we were missing Geordan and Drico, two big losses for any team. The idea was to put the ball in behind them and go from there. Saying that, we were only two points down in the second half at one stage. We could have won the game. That said, I don't think it was a game we should have won.'

Given the backdrop to the game, it was a defeat O'Sullivan could live with. 'I remember the night of the game. I've lost other games and been sick about it. I wasn't sick this time. OK, we lost by 18 points and there was a lot of negative reaction to it. I was disappointed and a bit niggled that we actually lost that game in five minutes of the second half but I was not at all down.

'We'd struggled for periods of the game but France are a good side. One of the things that struck me was that we'd lost the game because of basic errors which we don't normally make. I knew they were all fixable. If it had been a case of France being too strong, too quick, too powerful, there's not much you can do about it. But this was fixable. The other thing was our reaction. Traditionally in Paris, having given up two quick tries in succession, there'd be another five or six to follow and you'd be looking for a hole to jump into. We came back into it. We hadn't got it perfectly right but there were positive things coming out of the game. I saw it as a kind of a springboard for the Wales game.'

Wales, meanwhile, had obliterated Scotland, even if the final scoreline was only 23–10. Hadn't you heard about Wales? There was talk of a revival in the valleys.

Above: Gordon D'Arcy tests Damien Traille on the outside, with Frankie Sheahan in support. 'I just wanted the ball,' recalled D'Arcy. 'I just wanted to run.'

Below: Shane Byrne, who had sought assurances from the team management about his selection, scores his second try against Wales. Out of respect, Keith Wood donned a mullet wig that night.

Above: Would Brian O'Driscoll's hamstring be up to the demands of test rugby after a six-week lay-off? Ireland's captain removes all doubt by ploughing through the Welsh defence.

Left: Ronan O'Gara gets all balletic against Wales. For the second match in succession, O'Gara would begin and end the game as Ireland's out-half.

Right: A relaxed-looking Eddie O'Sullivan considers the prospect of taking on the world champions at Twickenham. Assistant coach Declan Kidney listens attentively.

Below: A star is reborn. D'Arcy torments the Welsh midfield defence yet again.

Above: Paul O'Connell ensures Ireland remain on the front foot against England despite the best efforts of Josh Lewsey, Trevor Woodman and Phil Vickery.

Left: Shane Byrne appears to be on the verge of kissing Girvan Dempsey after the match-winning try in Twickenham. Dempsey is in agony following Ben Cohen's studs-first slide into his knee.

Right, top: The tackle from the end of the earth. Despite Mark Regan's victory dance moments later, Malcolm O'Kelly knew it was no try. The video referee agreed.

Right, bottom: And then it was over. Shane Byrne, Keith Gleeson, Gordon D'Arcy, Ronan O'Gara and Kevin Maggs whoop it up.

Above: None of the Irish forwards were substituted at Twickenham – a rare occurrence in test rugby these days. Gleeson, Easterby and O'Connell are in no hurry to hit the showers.

Left: Brian O'Driscoll was sin binned for his tackle on Italy's scrum-half Paul Griffen, though this shot shows he was 'tackling the ball'.

Above: 'Only Wally could have got that score,' said Eddie O'Sullivan of the try that ended a nervous spell against Scotland at Lansdowne Road.

Below: Peter Stringer puts the matter beyond any doubt. Let the celebrations begin.

Above: The lap of honour. John Hayes, the original strong, silent type, allows himself to get wrapped up in the emotion of a special occasion.

Below: Coach and captain smile for the cameras.

CHAPTER 3 – WALES

RELEASE THE HOUNDS

Getting your rooming arrangements wrong can lead to trouble. Just ask Rudolf Straeuli, the former South African coach, who twinned locks Geo Cronje and Quinton Davids for a Springboks training camp before the 2003 World Cup. It was a marriage made in hell. Two men who were literally fighting for the same place – Cronje, the unreconstructed Afrikaner, complete with his *Voortrekker* beard, and Davids the 'Cape coloured'. When Cronje refused point blank to share the same shower as his rival, it sparked a controversy that raged for weeks, causing suspensions, resignations and a storm of ill-feeling. All because of a dodgy rooming list.

Things are slightly less volatile in the Irish camp but the rooming list is still something that needs to be got right. Joan Breslin, the IRFU's International Squad Administrator, decided on the pairings in conjunction with one of the players, rooming secretary David Humphreys. In the past, there may have been a political aspect to certain partnerships. Following a fiery exchange in the 2002 Celtic League final between Leinster and Munster, Eric Miller and Anthony Foley were paired together by the Irish management so they could sort out their differences. Two years later, the situation had changed. In World Cup year especially, Ireland's international players spent more time sleeping in hotel rooms than they did at home. The most important consideration – no, make that the only consideration – is that your roomie is someone you feel comfortable with. If that means Munster with Munster and Leinster with Leinster, then so be it.

Ronan O'Gara, for example, likes rooming with Alan Quinlan – both get wound up before test games but Quinlan's nervy sense of humour puts a smile on O'Gara's face. Quinlan was out injured for the Six Nations so O'Gara shared with Simon Easterby for the duration of the tournament. Both like to turn the light off early so they suited each other fine. Paul O'Connell enjoyed rooming with Foley because it meant he could pester him for 'old school' stories – he loves hearing all the boozy yarns from the amateur era. Humphreys, meanwhile, parked himself with Girvan Dempsey. No messing about with Girv, no high jinks. Just a solid night's kip.

When it came to finding a room-mate for Shane Byrne, there was one quality required – the candidate had to be able to put up with a pair of one-year-old twins occasionally rummaging through his personal effects. Kerry and Alex Byrne would make the odd visit to Citywest or to the Radisson Hotel in Stillorgan, where the squad based itself the day before games at Lansdowne Road. They could cause quite a bit of damage in a short amount of time. Fortunately, there was someone who didn't mind in the slightest.

After what he'd been through in the previous four years, Gordon D'Arcy could put up with just about anything except rejection. His was the classic tale of too much too young. He'd been preparing for his Leaving Certificate back in 1998 when a phone call came through from Warren Gatland to see whether he'd fancy a tour to South Africa with the senior Ireland squad. In retrospect, he bore a certain resemblance to English football's wunderkind, Wayne Rooney – immature, slightly overweight, jaw-droppingly talented but in need of minding. The folks at Clongowes Wood reckoned it was a bad idea so he stayed at home to do his exams. By the following year, however, he'd made his international debut in the Rugby World Cup, aged 19. At the time, we could only guess at how many more caps he'd win before the next one came around in 2003.

The next World Cup came around and he'd won, er, five caps, all of them off the bench in what amounted to friendly games. D'Arcy's sense of frustration was unbearable – and not just for himself. To Alan Gaffney, Leinster's assistant coach for a couple of seasons, D'Arcy could be '... a pain in the hole, to be honest. I just thought, "Who is this upstart?"' Matt Williams, putting it more euphemistically, said D'Arcy needed some 'tough love'. He got it in spades.

It looked like it might work too. D'Arcy played a full 'A' international championship in a new, experimental role at outside centre – O'Sullivan didn't deem the experiment a success but his form and versatility surely meant he was in the frame for the World Cup squad of 30, to be announced in early September. All he needed was a decent tour of Samoa and Tonga in June. It didn't happen. He knew he was struggling when he failed to start either test match and drew no further encouragement when he made another appearance off the bench in a World Cup warm-up game against Wales. That said, he couldn't bear the notion of being told he wouldn't be going to Australia, so he left his mobile phone switched off on the morning of Sunday, 7 September, the day O'Sullivan would name his 30 players.

'I didn't want a call,' he said. 'I turned my phone off and got a voice message because I just couldn't deal with it. I woke up at around midday and got my message – "You're not going. You're in the shadow squad." I didn't know what to think. I knew coming up to selection that it wasn't going my way but the sudden fact of it really opened my eyes. I rang my mum to tell her and all the emotions that had been building up for the previous six months ended up just pouring out. There I was, bawling down the phone to my mum. I suppose that's what mums are for.'

There was sympathy at Leinster too. D'Arcy turned up for training the next day and his coach, Gary Ella, just shook his head. 'Jesus, mate, did you do something you shouldn't have done?' He was told to take two days off, to get his head straight. By the time he turned up for training on the Wednesday, he had done just that. He had one more year on his IRFU contract so he'd give it his all. If nothing came of it, he'd go abroad, maybe give up rugby altogether. Whatever happened, there'd be no more agonising, no more regrets. 'There are only so many times you can pick yourself up off the ground. You use people to pick yourself up – your parents, coaches and so on. They tell you you're great and that you'll get there. There's only so much of that you can take. I knew in my heart of hearts, this was going

Brian O'Driscoll's hamstring came as a blow for just about everybody in or around the Irish rugby team – except Gordon D'Arcy. He grabbed his unexpected chance with both hands.

to be the last time that I was going to be able to take the disappointment. It was just getting too much to take. So yes, I would have weighed up my options a lot more seriously. In the end, I just got on with it. With everyone else away at the World Cup, I was the most senior guy playing for Leinster by about 30 caps so there was a little bit of responsibility. I got to play eight or nine games at full-back which I hadn't done in four years. I just got to play rugby. Gary never once said I couldn't do this or that. He never once put any boundaries on my game. "Just go play rugby," he said. I thought, Nice one.

'Then Drico goes and gets injured, and in his typical laid-back way, Gary asked what did I think about playing thirteen for the game away to Sale. It's not that I was keen on the idea or not keen. I've always thought that if a coach asks you do something, you respond. I think I did. Like my defence that day – I'd about four tackles on Jason Robinson, which is a lot for any-body in one game on that guy. I caught him twice in open-field coun-terattacks, so I was very happy. Gary had faith in me and everything seemed to click into place.'

It would still take Eddie O'Sullivan time to have the same faith. O'Sullivan had been at an International Rugby Board (IRB) conference in Auckland the weekend D'Arcy ran amok in Sale and although he watched the video on his return, he needed more convincing. He'd never been sure about D'Arcy, knew he had talent but thought he lacked consistency. But the more he saw, the more convinced he became. Leinster played Cardiff at home and Biarritz away and on both occasions, D'Arcy looked like an inter-national centre. Starting him in Paris was risky and O'Sullivan is not a risk-taker by nature. But all his game breakers were gone – O'Driscoll, Denis Hickie and Geordan Murphy. D'Arcy's form demanded inclusion.

The player himself was happy just to be named in the squad of 22. It was with wide-eyed pleasure he picked up his kitbag at Citywest on the Sunday. His mind was racing. Would it be Shane Horgan at thirteen and maybe him-self on the wing? It didn't matter. He'd be involved in some way and that was all that counted. He was 'dumbfounded' when O'Sullivan revealed his team to the players on the Tuesday morning before the game.

15 Girvan Dempsey

14 Shane Horgan

13 Gordon D'Arcy

You f***ing beauty, he thought. The rest of the team – and the rest of the day – was a blur.

O'Sullivan shielded him from the press in order to keep his mind on the job at hand. 'Eddie was protective of me and I think that was where our relationship started to evolve a little bit,' said D'Arcy. 'He told me to keep out of the papers, because if I was all over the papers, I was only building myself up for a fall. He told me to keep concentrating on the game but not to get overawed by it. He just kept giving me little bits of information every now and again, never overloading the system. Obviously I was up against a big guy in [Yannick] Jauzion but that didn't worry me at all. He's actually only half a stone heavier than me and he's got to get down to get me. [Damien] Traille is the guy I was worried about. He's one of the best footballers in the world. He makes things happen for people outside him. So I was a bit worried about him but I just wanted the ball. I wanted to run.'

D'Arcy only got a couple of opportunities to run in Paris but he made one of them pay. That half-break and off-load to Tyrone Howe in the final quarter was an *amuse bouche* before the more substantial dishes to be served later in the tournament. At the time, he wasn't sure whether he'd done enough to hold his place – the word from the team's medical staff was that Brian O'Driscoll would be ready for Wales at Lansdowne Road the following Sunday. There was no point in worrying, however. He'd finally started a game for Ireland and acquitted himself well. He was pretty relaxed as he and Byrne unpacked back at Citywest.

On the face of it, they were an odd couple. There are separated by seven years and by musical taste – an important consideration when you're sharing a room with someone for two months. Whereas D'Arcy favours 'chill-out' sounds, Byrne likes heavy metal (which might just explain one of the more famous hairstyles in world rugby). He went to see Iron Maiden when they played in Dublin, even inveigled a few Leinster team-mates along. D'Arcy was not one of them.

Yet the two former boarders were well-matched in other respects. 'Strange as it may seem, we have a lot in common,' said D'Arcy. 'We like the same TV shows. We used to get up and stick on *Stargate* at 8.30 in the morning. We'd just sit there and chill out. Occasionally he'd bring the twins into the room so I got my blast of reality. My watch would disappear into a mouth or one of them would be sucking on my boot. After a while I barely noticed.'

Byrne had the twins visit as often as is practical. He is the first to admit, however, that international rugby is not good for family life. He was one of just four married men in the 2004 team (the others were David Humphreys, Reggie Corrigan and Anthony Foley) and Humphreys is the only other dad. The constant training and touring of the Irish rugby team can cause domestic strain.

'We all met our wives during the amateur era – I don't think the professional era lends itself to relationships,' he laughed. 'I can understand people would think there is a glamorous side to international sport and yes, there are nice bits to it. But the majority is horrible for family life. In the first year of my kids' lives, there were only two occasions when I was home for seven days in a row. I missed their birthday. I've never been home for a wedding anniversary either, or for Caroline's birthday – which is also Valentine's Day. Coming back from the World Cup last November, the kids didn't have a clue who I was, not a clue. Things like that are very hard. There's no-one who can give you advice on that either. It can be very stressful. Caroline had to finish work so she's at home all the time. Her family is from Monaghan, mine is from Wicklow and we live in Dublin. She understands an international career is relatively short, especially when you start late, like I did. But it can still be stressful.'

It wasn't the only stress Byrne was feeling in February 2004. Like D'Arcy, he had a point to prove. As Keith Wood's hooking understudy at the World Cup, he was next in line when The Great One retired. But Leinster were struggling and Frankie Sheahan, his main rival, had been in flying form for Munster. Wood then added some spice when asked by *Rugby World* magazine about the relative merits of Byrne and Sheahan. Sheahan, Wood said, was '... a lot bigger, a stronger scrummager, probably more effective around the field. His ruck and tackle count might be higher as well.' Byrne wasn't altogether surprised to read this – Wood and Sheahan were two Munstermen after all, while his own relationship with Wood had never been other than business-like. He just worried that O'Sullivan was thinking the same way. He decided to try and find out. 'For God's sake I was s****ing myself. Things weren't going well with Leinster and they were going better with Munster. It's always a hair's breadth between myself and Frankie anyway. So I was a really nervous man and I reckon because of that, I didn't play my best game against France. I was thinking too much about it, being careful not to make mistakes. You can't play international rugby like that. It was getting so crazy that I had to go and talk to a few people in the management team about it. I didn't know whether I was coming or going or what the story was. I was basically just told what's going to happen is going to happen and not to be bloody worrying about it. I got a vote of confidence but I was still fretting when the team for Wales was read out. You're still wondering was there something I didn't do right? You're just glad when you hear "Number two, Shane Byrne." You're thinking, Thank you, God, thank you.'

There was a general edginess in the camp. Maybe it was all the talk about Wales's performance in Cardiff the previous Saturday, maybe it was the uncertainty over team selection. Whatever it was, Monday's training at Naas RFC was a narky affair. O'Sullivan went back to basics, separating the players into two teams, throwing the ball up in the air and letting them get on with it. 'It was pretty brutal,' recalled Mike Ford, the defence coach. 'I remember it well. A fight broke out, it was that physical. I don't think we planned it that way but it set the tone for the week.'

The Monday night video show wasn't a bundle of laughs either. This is a practice Ford has brought from his days as a rugby league pro for Wigan, Castleford, Warrington and Great Britain, whereby the faults of the most recent performance are pinpointed before the entire team, often with painful precision. 'It's taken time to be able to do that,' said Ford. 'The environment beforehand wouldn't allow it because certain players wouldn't have been able to handle it. So we had to bring it in gradually. We've got to a situation now where I can pinpoint players now in front of their peers, which can be unpleasant. The videos are such these days that you just can't hide. If you're in a ruck and the ball's gone three passes away from you, I'm still watching to see if you've got off the ground quickly. And the players know that I'm watching. There's nowhere to hide.

'I had it myself in rugby league, with Darryl van der Weld, an Aussie who used to coach me at Castleford. He was pretty frank in the video room and you just didn't want to be the star of the Monday night video.

'It meant you understood the game better and maybe a little quicker too. I take the defence video and Eddie does attack. We're not tearing the lads to bits. We're not having a go at their attitude or their enthusiasm. It's just that you can't afford to let up at international level for one second. If you make a mistake, you're going to pay the price.'

As Ford said, these video nasties did take a bit getting used to for the players. 'I kinda struggled with it when I went up to the national team at first,' said Paul O'Connell. 'I was thinking, Why can't they be more positive with people? I'd only been a professional for six months and I was coming from Munster where Deccy [Declan Kidney] and Niallo [forwards coach Niall O'Donovan] were easing me into things. Next minute you're up with Ireland and when you drop a ball, you're told to raise your standard. At first, you're there thinking, Jesus, calm down a bit. But we're at the highest level now. If there are 30 people in the video room and Mike Ford has the red beam on you as you're leaving pillar from a ruck and being dinked, you will not do it again the next game. I'm all for that.'

There were a few men reddened by Ford's beam that Monday evening. For Pascal Papé's try, both Malcolm O'Kelly and Shane Horgan got themselves isolated ahead of the defensive line. Five minutes later, John Hayes made a similar mistake and Yannick Jauzion was in. That was 14 points in five minutes. Someone would surely pay with his place.

Malcolm O'Kelly felt particularly vulnerable. Donncha O'Callaghan had been flying for Munster, drawing rave reviews from one Clive Woodward in the process. He had also played the last 20 minutes in Paris, which Ireland had spent mostly on the front foot. O'Donovan had already informed O'Kelly that O'Sullivan was a little unhappy with his performance in Paris, so, in a way, he was expecting the worst. It still came as a surprise to the general public, however, if only for the fact that O'Kelly was such an established player. He had won his sixtieth cap in Paris and was now being replaced by someone who had only made his international debut the previous year. O'Sullivan's explanation gave a clue as to the mental approach he was trying to instil for what then looked like the pivotal game of Ireland's tournament. 'It spices things up a little in the tight five. Donncha plays with a certain amount of abandon and throws his body around. It's a tight call but I think he's ready for it.'

O'Kelly's omission wasn't the only bombshell that Tuesday morning. Kevin Maggs, only one cap behind O'Kelly on 59 and a cast-iron selection for the previous 12 months, had also been axed. Ireland would play against Wales with O'Driscoll and D'Arcy together in the centre – for the first time at any level of the game.

O'Driscoll, who had been chosen slightly out of position at inside centre, was sanguine, however. 'It's very exciting,' he said. 'D'Arce has been the in-form back in the Heineken Cup. At centre he probably doesn't have as much time to think as in the back three and he just lets his footballing ability take over. I don't think we even trained together in the centre before but he's playing with an incredible amount of confidence at the moment.'

It wasn't a confidence shared by everyone in the media pack. It would be nice to say we saw what was coming but it would also be untrue. To a man (and one woman – Orla Bannon of the *Irish Mirror*) we predicted it would be close. In a sense, we wanted it to be close. It would be a better story that way. The championship needed more close-run affairs. Ireland had shaken things up by nearly beating France in '98 and '99, then actually beating them in 2000 and '01. It was still effectively a two-tier championship, however. For the good of the tournament and for the good of journalists everywhere, Wales needed to join Ireland on the mezzanine level.

As far as the Welsh public was concerned – and according to the legendary J P R Williams – they were already there. Hadn't they given both New Zealand and England a bit of a fright at the World Cup? Hadn't they wiped the floor with Scotland the previous week, scoring three scintillating tries in the process? We joined in on the hysteria being whipped up in the Welsh media, conveniently downplaying a couple of salient facts. First, they hadn't beaten either New Zealand or England at the World Cup. Second,

Scotland's defence in Cardiff had been lamentable. But did we really care? You couldn't mention Wales without applying the adjective 'resurgent' and that was all there was to it.

All we can now claim is some small part in Ireland's motivational process. 'The previews for the Wales game said more about the media than about the team,' said John Redmond. 'The Welsh revival was a better story. In fact, the pre-championship angle was all too convenient. Admittedly the challenge facing us was a tough one but it was all doom and gloom. We're going to get beaten in Paris and London and, in between that, there's Wales, who should have won the World Cup by all accounts. We were looking down the barrel. It was typical. There's a sense amongst the players that if there's 50/50 call to be made, the Irish media will always go for the other team. It should have been dispiriting but it wasn't. The Welsh were believing their own press, while we were defiant of ours.'

The comments of the players bear this out. 'We'd taken a good shoeing from France in a 10-minute period and lost the game because of that,' said Reggie Corrigan. 'Then we came back to this barrage. There was a huge amount of hype and bullshit all week about Wales and how they were back. In fairness, there was a thin margin between it being an amazing season and the worst season for years. But I think a lot of guys took it as a bit of an insult that the Welsh thought they could rock into town and be this new force. As provinces, we wouldn't fear any of the Welsh teams in the Celtic League or the European Cup. So what's different between the best of them against the best of us? Why would they suddenly be that much better? That's the question we kept asking ourselves. And as the week went on, they kept getting built up more and more. It was perfect for us, it really was. They kept feeding us the scraps that we needed.'

Paul O'Connell felt the same way. 'Wales at home? They'd had a couple of reasonable games but we always knew if we played well we'd beat them. Like, we hadn't lost to them for a good few years and we saw our-selves as at least the third-best team in the championship behind England and France, by a long way. Next minute, Wales are coming to Lansdowne

Road as favourites, which is a bit typical of journalists when it comes to Ireland. They don't really believe in us. As soon as Wales come back a little bit, next minute they're better than us. I suppose it was a motivating factor all right.'

It wasn't just the forwards who were geeing themselves up. The backs had heard enough about their Welsh counterparts and were itching to get at them too, none more so than O'Driscoll. Having been out of action for six weeks, he was brimming with boyish enthusiasm at the eve-of-match press conference at Lansdowne Road. A Welsh journalist asked how he would cope with the threat of Welsh centre, Iestyn Harris. 'By getting up in his face and smashing him,' said O'Driscoll, a response that brought a smile from Eddie O'Sullivan sitting alongside.

As for Wales coach Steve Hansen, he was more concerned with the threat posed by Brian O'Driscoll. During the week, he detailed a couple of Welsh journalists to try and find out whether O'Driscoll would actually be playing – clearly he suspected, or rather hoped his inclusion was a smokescreen. As it turned out, his fears were justified.

First there was the Shane Byrne Show, however. It was the most unlikely beginning to a test match – within 60 seconds, the Magic Mullet was jogging back to the halfway line, his face one vast smile. The simplicity of the score was a little deceptive. For starters, it was easy to take for granted the accuracy of O'Gara's kickoff, deep into the Welsh 22 with a gale at his back – to be sure of forcing an Irish line-out, his target area was relatively tiny. From there, it was all about the controlled aggression of the Irish maul.

'That was just an incredible experience,' said Byrne. 'It was a sweet catch in the line-out by Simon Easterby and all of the guys did superb work up in front of me. It was textbook mauling and the space just opened up. Anthony Foley, who was beside me, spotted it before I did. He was screaming at me, "GO! GO!" Then I did that lovely stylish dive to the ground. OK, so it wasn't the best. I just wasn't knocking that ball on, no flipping way.'

We waited for Wales to regroup and then show us what all the hype had been about. It never happened. What we got instead was one of the biggest

Astonishingly, there were less than 60 seconds on the clock when Shane Byrne touched down for the first time. Stephen Jones and Iestyn Harris look accusingly at the Welsh forwards.

anticlimaxes imaginable. Welsh out-half Stephen Jones did put his side on the scoreboard with a penalty but soon O'Driscoll was wriggling through some desperately poor defending to lunge over the line. O'Gara followed up his own charge-down to add a third try and then Byrne burrowed over for his second, off another line-out maul. It was 24–3 at the break. Maybe Wales would be better with the wind at their backs. Not a bit of it. Their defence for Foley's try was risible. First O'Gara sent O'Driscoll through a gaping hole with a simple switch move and then Peter Stringer's snipe drew Sonny Parker away from his position as pillar – an unforgivable error at this

Ronan O'Gara follows up his block-down of Iestyn Harris's attempted clearance for Ireland's third try and already, midway through the first half, the game had run away from Wales.

level. O'Driscoll completed the carnage after yet another line-break, this time by Keith Gleeson. It was embarrassingly easy.

It wasn't entirely perfect, mind. Ireland did concede a couple of soft tries to Tom Shanklin in the final quarter, making for a misleading final score of 36–15. There was also misfortune for O'Callaghan, whose first test start had been spoiled by a knee ligament strain which forced him off just before half-time and allowed O'Kelly a reprieve. On a lighter note, Girvan Dempsey had also received a yellow card for obstruction five minutes from time, which was entirely unwarranted. First of all, the player was entitled to challenge for the ball as he did. Secondly, the player in question was Tyrone Howe, who fled the scene of the 'crime' as soon as he suspected there was a flag on the play. Dempsey's team-mates got a giggle out of that – the model student getting the blame for something he didn't do.

Wales coach Steve Hansen had his spies out in force to find out whether Brian O'Driscoll would really be returning from injury. Bad news, Steve.

It was a minor blemish. Resurgent Wales had been put back in their box. O'Driscoll had made a successful return to top-flight rugby, scoring twice in the process. The pack had not only handled the Welsh forwards, they had given them a good spanking. Mike Ford's defensive analysis, which included deploying a couple of tacklers in the outside centre channel, had worked a treat. Ronan O'Gara, whose relationship with the Irish number ten shirt had been of the hokey-cokey variety, had closed out two games in a row. Shane Byrne, the man who felt it necessary to get assurances over his security of tenure, had scored two tries. Out of respect, Keith Wood was forced to wear a mullet wig on *Rugby Special* that Sunday evening.

Yet the man they were all talking about hadn't scored, hadn't even finished the game. Gordon D'Arcy had to be replaced after 58 minutes because of a bruised hip but he was still the talk of the tournament. His astonishing footwork had upended both Rhys Williams and Martyn Williams, the latter resorting to a foot-trip in desperation. Almost as striking was the amount of defensive dirty work he was getting through with O'Driscoll. It was a match made in rugby heaven. As D'Arcy said: 'Myself and Brian played against each other in school so we've always known each other. We played for the Leinster reserve team together, when nobody knew who we were, and when we were both crap, incidentally. We've always had the same mentality – get the ball and go for it. The fact that we're similar in physique means running styles are the same and I can read what he's doing and vice versa. It's nice to play off someone who has the same mentality as you. When Eddie picked us, we didn't think in terms of fixed roles. The numbers on our backs didn't really mean anything. If I want to run a move, I run it, and if he wants to run a move, he runs it. If he wants to put in a few hits, he goes to inside centre, or I can do the same. It's great being able to swap.' Brian asked did he mind if he wore number thirteen, as he'd never worn another number for Ireland. 'Did I care? I was playing for Ireland, for God's sake.

'We both love the defensive stuff. We had little competitions to see who can win more ball on the ground. I think he won 3–2 in the Welsh game. Out on the wing or at full-back, you're not a groundhog, you're going full tilt to catch the other guy, who's also going at full tilt. If you hit him, you're both struggling to recover quickly. There's no winning the ball. At thirteen, you're closer to the tackle. So when Brian hits someone, I'm straight in on the ball. And we seemed to work well in attack too. Because I was making a few holes, defenders now had to look at me. They couldn't now keep both eyes on Drico, they could only keep half an eye on him. It meant he got a little more time on the ball.'

It was a partnership formed entirely by chance, and owed a lot to Gary Ella, incidentally. O'Sullivan, you'll recall, had tried D'Arcy as an outside centre in the previous year's 'A' championship and hadn't deemed the experiment a success. Did he care? The dreaded possibility of travelling to

Twickenham after two defeats had been averted. And the coach admitted that this possibility had crossed his mind once or twice.

'I bought into the Welsh revival stuff to a certain extent,' O Sullivan said. 'I thought Steve Hansen had brought them a long way. I'm a good friend of Hansen, I've a lot of time for him. He had a difficult time trying to get certain things in place which would be of benefit in the long term and I think the World Cup proved that. But the Welsh media got carried away when they beat Scotland. They now believed that they had turned the corner and got everything right. They'd turned the corner all right but they hadn't got as far round it as they thought. I felt that they were actually a bit ahead of themselves. This was the way I put it to our guys. At the front of the Welsh players' minds, they were believing what they're reading in their own press; but in the back of their mind, there must be some lingering doubts. When you think of it, really they'd only won one game. The key for us was to bring what was in the back of their mind to the front of their mind. The best way to do that was to get into them physically early on. We needed to release the hounds.

'I didn't bank on us scoring within 60 seconds but that was the plan – to get into them early. Wales can be as physical as anyone but what I read into their build-up is that they were actually thinking more about their easy yards than the hard yards. Hansen knew going into that game that they weren't quite where the media had placed them but he couldn't do anything abut it. The media had got hold of it. So I felt it was all about throwing down markers early in the game. Wales can play fantastic rugby if they're give space and time. If we ended up in a game like that, we mightn't have won it. It was about getting our retaliation in first, if you like. The way it happened couldn't have been better. They were shocked when we scored and then suddenly we had scored again. When they tried to come at us, we turned them over again and again – in fairness to Mike Ford, he read their game really well. I thought we got the build-up right and we got the game plan right.'

As for Hansen, he was surely reminded of what his predecessor, Graham

Henry, had said about the capricious Welsh rugby public: 'When they win, the players are welcomed as world beaters. When they lose, they're afraid to go out of their houses.' The way Hansen put it was apt enough. It was, he said, '... a case of the young guns trying to poke their noses in with the big boys. They got a good slap.' O'Sullivan might have phrased it another way. The Welsh had had their asses served to them on a plate.

CHAPTER 4 – ENGLAND
PARTY POOPERS

'I thought we'd win. I was feeling nowhere near as confident as during the
World Cup but I still thought we'd win.' – Clive Woodward.

Even before Ireland had taken the field against Wales on that bright,
blustery Sunday in February, Eddie O'Sullivan had received one piece
of good news. Bill Beaumont, manager of the 2005 British and Irish Lions
confirmed to *The Sunday Tribune* that O'Sullivan would be part of Clive
Woodward's coaching team for the tour to New Zealand. 'It's down to
Clive, but based on the conversations we've had, he'd be interested in
having Eddie on board in some capacity. He's got a lot to offer,' said
Beaumont.

At first glance, the pair did not seem well matched. Woodward is the
visionary behind England's World Cup triumph, known for impetuous ges-
tures and occasional histrionics; O'Sullivan is the cool pragmatist. Woodward
does a victory dance when his team scores a try; O'Sullivan's body lan-
guage in similar circumstances is restrained. Then there was the power
thing. How would Eddie take to being a subordinate all over again? Everyone knew he had been a little uncomfortable as number two to Warren
Gatland. Sir Clive doesn't have a reputation as being an easy man to work
for either.

In fact, they have a sound relationship. O'Sullivan's first encounter with
Woodward was back to 1997, when they coached their respective countries' Under-21 teams. Ireland beat England 28–27 at Greystones that year,
thanks to a last-minute try by David Wallace. Woodward had much the

better of their next two head-to-heads, however. In 2002, England beat Ireland 45–11 at Twickenham, O'Sullivan's second game in charge of the senior side. The following year, Woodward's side walloped Ireland 42–6 in the Grand Slam decider at Lansdowne Road. That evening, when the two men compared notes at the post-match banquet, Woodward commented that Ireland were two years behind England. It might have sounded arrogant but it was meant it as a compliment. O'Sullivan took it as one too.

Not everyone in the Ireland camp was able to remain quite so calm that night. Mike Ford remembers a conversation with Jason Robinson, a fellow league convert, who asked Ford where he had expected England's attacking threat to come from. 'I told him it didn't matter what I'd thought, now that they'd put six tries past us,' said Ford. 'They were just a little smug that evening. That's the way I perceived it anyway. I just didn't think it was the right time to be asking questions like that. I just banked it for a later date.'

O'Sullivan was hurting too but he was ready to chalk it down to experience. He's the first to admit that England laid down standards for all northern hemisphere sides. England were first to tap into rugby league defensive systems under Phil Larder, first to employ specialist coaches for individual skills like kicking and line-out throwing. They were ahead of the game in terms of video technology and physical conditioning as well. They had stumbled occasionally along the way, but Woodward had always seen the bigger picture. And he got his reward on 22 November 2003 when Martin Johnson lifted the Webb Ellis Trophy at the Telstra Stadium in Sydney. O'Sullivan applauded as loudly as anyone.

By the time the Six Nations came around, Woodward didn't want to hear any more about the World Cup. Enough had been said and written. The Webb Ellis Trophy – now known simply as 'Bill' – had been paraded from John O'Groats to Land's End, it seemed. As of New Year's Day, he didn't want to see it or hear about it again. It was time to move on.

But where to? How could he improve upon the system? Woodward tried to keep things fresh on and off the pitch. He experimented with Jason Robinson at outside centre. There was talk of using an aromatherapist in the dressing room. The subtle release of scents like basil, peppermint and citrus oil might make the players even more alert, he argued, much to the confusion of Bernard Laporte, the French coach. 'What do these odours have to do with rugby? I have never heard anything like it!' Woodward also employed a visual awareness specialist to improve the players' 'peripheral vision'.

It appeared that he was becoming too preoccupied with the peripheral, however. He seemed distracted. The Scots were out to get him, for one thing. The day before England's 35–13 win in Edinburgh (the same weekend as Wales were in Dublin), he complained about the surface moisture on the pitch at Murrayfield, hinting it had been watered deliberately in order to reduce his team's effectiveness. He didn't like the feng shui in the visitors' dressing room either. A large pillar in the middle of the room 'screwed things up'. And this is before we got to the pre-match festivities.

'Firework Phil' Anderton, the Scottish Rugby Union's marketing guru (and subsequently its chief executive), had arranged quite a pageant, involving 300 pipers and highland dancers, lots of noise and lots of smoke. There was a total of 15 minutes from the time that the England players left their ill-designed dressing room to the game actually starting. The Scots, having won the toss, also left their guests guessing as to which direction they would be playing. Woodward was justifiably upset. 'The worst places to come to are Murrayfield and Lansdowne Road – they seem to delight in it,' he said. 'Teams spend half their time trying to wind us up but it actually has the opposite effect.'

No sooner was Woodward back on home soil than he was taking umbrage at a comment attributed to Brian O'Driscoll in the media. Ireland, O'Driscoll hoped, might make the Twickenham faithful 'choke on their prawn sandwiches' – a playful allusion to a famous Roy Keane-ism. To Woodward, however, it was an unnecessary slight on England's rugby supporters. A month later, when he generously agreed to be interviewed for this book, he still wasn't impressed. 'I was a bit surprised, personally, that a player of his reputation would make those kind of comments. I don't think

After England's World Cup triumph, Clive Woodward probably knew the only way
was down. He could hardly have known the fall would be so sudden, however.

it affected the result. I think our team had gone beyond that. I think he was
a bit out of line, there. Funnily enough, I watched the game again afterwards and I don't think O'Driscoll had one of his better games. Maybe he
was thinking too much about the prawn sandwiches.' Miaow.

As it happens, O'Driscoll now protests his innocence, even though he's
amused at the reaction he got. 'I heard Clive's outburst. He had a big old
bite. I was trying to think back as to when I'd actually said it. It was probably taken completely out of context or two quotes were stuck together as
often happens. When you're talking, occasionally something stupid comes
out of your mouth. It was just one of those cases. I wouldn't plan that. I'm
not that sort of person at all. I don't play the media game. I leave that to

others. I just like to get on with the business. This was something I said innocently that got blown out of all proportion. I never intended to offend anyone. You certainly don't need to give England any ammunition.'

It's not as though the Red Rose Brigade were lacking motivation. Two workaday performances had accounted for Italy and Scotland, both on the road. Here was the homecoming. True, 'Bill' wouldn't be making an appearance, and Woodward insisted there be no pre-match pyrotechnics. But it was still England's homecoming. What an occasion.

They did have problems. Martin Johnson and Jonny Wilkinson, their two most influential players at the World Cup, were missing – one retired, the other injured. Charlie Hodgson, Woodward's second-choice out-half, was also out. There was even an admission from within the camp that winning consecutive grand slams was a dizzyingly tall order. 'We won the World Cup and that's great but we went through without playing to the potential of the team,' said Lawrence Dallaglio, Johnson's successor as captain, to *The Guardian*. 'You don't mind how you win but, if we're honest, we probably played better rugby before the World Cup than we did during it. Everyone plays well against England and now the stakes are even higher ... The first defeat, when it comes, is going to be big news.'

England's team announcement brought big news for O'Sullivan. Mike Tindall hadn't recovered sufficiently from injury so Robinson would remain out of position at centre while Iain Balshaw would stay at full-back, where he had been exposed at Lansdowne Road three years previously. The return of Matt Dawson was a worry but both Danny Grewcock and Simon Shaw were out injured. This reduced their beef quota and deprived them of a specialist front jumper – Ben Kay and Steve Borthwick formed the second row. Without Neil Back, now demoted, their back row of Dallaglio, Joe Worsley and Richard Hill also lacked a specialist open-side. Ireland, meanwhile, showed just one change – O'Kelly was back in for the injured O'Callaghan.

Later, after England had been beaten, Woodward's insistence on playing players out of position would be interpreted as arrogance, even by those within the English game. Gloucester coach Nigel Melville saw it thus: 'So far in the Six Nations Championship, England seemed to think that all they needed to do was get their best 15 players on the pitch, no matter whether they were playing out of position, and that would see them through; individual talent would out ... In almost every tier of the side put out against Ireland there were guys playing out of position. It showed.'

Was this arrogance on Woodward's part? We'd probably like to think so because it fits neatly into a historical pattern wherein Irish teams supposedly perform best when they have been slighted by Englishmen – Dick Greenwood in 1985, Geoff Cooke in 1994. We look for the slightest hint of self-satisfaction and with the wisdom of hindsight, we attribute enormous importance to it.

As they entered their dressing room, a few Irish players noticed the plaques arranged around the frame of the door – 22 of them to signify each of England's consecutive wins at Twickenham. That irked them slightly. Then they may very well have spotted England's Six Nations 'menu' printed in the match programmes placed in each cubicle – Italy for starter, Scotland Ireland and Wales as entrées and finally France for dessert. That could sound presumptuous, if you wanted it to.

These details are mere footnotes to the main script, however. And that script, prepared in fine detail by Eddie O'Sullivan, Mike Ford, Niall O'Donovan, Declan Kidney and video analyst Mervyn Murphy, was the basis for what would follow, nothing else. Ireland got the game plan right. From that point on, they had a chance.

'We put a lot of work into knowing how we wanted to play against them,' said O'Sullivan. 'We targeted their set piece, looked to upset their line-out in particular. In defence, we looked to make a lot more impact tackles, where the ball carrier is stopped dead or knocked backwards. That would stop them off-loading in the tackle. We knew there would be times when they'd come at us in certain places. We'd have certain numbers there – we'd take the ball off them or at least stop them. In attack, we wouldn't try and go to the outside channels as early, as we'd done at Lansdowne Road

Mike Ford and Eddie O'Sullivan. After what he'd seen – and heard – the last time Ireland played England, Ford went to Twickenham intent on vengeance.

the previous year. We'd play our way into the game, a bit like a batsman, not try and beat them in the first 10 minutes. We'd put the ball in the corners early on, try and turn them, take the momentum out of their game, make sure the score was still pretty tight after 20 minutes.'

'I can remember when I realised we'd a great opportunity,' said Ford. 'I was at home in Oldham the Saturday before the game, looking at videos of England's games against Italy and Scotland. I saw how oppositions tend to stand off England and let them play. They like to go to the middle of the pitch and then have options to go left or right. But what would happen if you stopped them in the middle, didn't allow them to go wide? I just got this goosey feeling all over. I knew no-one would back us. It was the perfect opportunity.'

Setting it up is pretty scientific. O'Sullivan demanded a total of less than 40 'system errors' – this could be a wrong decision in defence, if not a missed tackle. Ford demanded a tackle efficiency rate in excess of 90 percent (as it turned out, he got 94 percent against England). There had to be passion too. It's an incredibly aggressive contact sport. It's England v Ireland. But the game has gone past the stage where teams are tearing opposition jerseys to shreds in the dressing room beforehand, turning the lights off and knocking heads together. It's all about quiet intensity these days.

The Irish players did consider one small psychological trick. 'There was talk of us clapping England onto the pitch as world champions,' said Malcolm O'Kelly. 'In fairness, Eddie is the kind of character who's always thinking. He thought we'd do it the way Young Munster do it, you know, clap a team out and then go and get stuck into them. It was only a suggestion, though, and, to be honest, I didn't think it was a good idea. We could have opened ourselves up if we had been beaten badly, which was always a possibility at Twickenham. It might have looked like we'd been in awe of them. To be honest, I just didn't want to clap these people out. It's not something I'd do. It could play havoc with your mind.'

O'Kelly had had enough playing on his mind for the previous few weeks. His problems had begun in Lanzarote, of course, with that no-show for the final day of training. When the news got out, it seemed to fit the perception of Big Mal as someone who exists in his own time zone, a place where there are 'no worries, buddy'. It's a perception that annoys him somewhat, especially given that he had worked hard that week.

'In fairness, I trained really hard and did absolutely everything that was asked of me,' he recalled. 'Then of course, the final night we had a bonding session. A man of my experience should know that you can't be late no matter what state you're in. You go and do your bit. I got a phone call to get out of bed from Liam Hennessy [national fitness director], who's actually a very soft-spoken guy, a good man, but I could sense a bit of anger in his voice. Myself and Anthony [Horgan] went downstairs but found there was nobody at the appointed place. Between the pair of us, we decided it wasn't Liam Hennessy who had rung us at all. We decided it was a wind-up and we should go back to bed. So we went back to bed. The next thing we knew, Liam was hammering on the door. He wasn't happy.' Neither was O'Sullivan.

O'Kelly's timing had been off in a few ways. Given Mike McGurn's incendiary comments on fitness training structures, the last thing the management needed was the public getting the impression that a fitness week had turned into a piss-up. Like Shane Byrne, O'Kelly also happened to have a rival who was playing in a thriving Munster side. He was told his suspension wouldn't affect team selection, but at the same time he was starting the championship on the back foot. While he felt he played well in Paris, he knew what was coming.

The way he and O'Callaghan handled the changing of the guard says something for the spirit within the Irish squad. On the Wednesday after Paris, the two of them went out for a meal near Citywest together with Paul O'Connell and Mick O'Driscoll, the former Munster lock who was home on a few days' holidays from Perpignan, his new club. O'Callaghan's face – and unruly locks – had been all over the newspapers that day. He received abuse all evening for the state of his mane: here he was, replacing someone who had been practically a first-choice for Ireland since 1997 – couldn't he afford to make himself presentable? The constant mock-admonishment served to lighten the mood.

It was still hard not to consider the possibility that it might all be over. O'Kelly had 60 caps, the guts of seven seasons in the front line and would be 30 the following summer. Fortunately there were people willing to encourage – Declan Kidney for one, despite the fact that they had never had a proper conversation before. Willie Anderson, then the forwards coach at Leinster, also got in touch. It meant that O'Kelly was in the right mental state when O'Callaghan's injury gave him an unexpected reprieve.

'Declan gave me a line on which to travel,' said O'Kelly. 'He said I could curl up in a ball, like I might have done in the past, or I could do something about it. I opened myself up to him a lot. In fairness he'd taken a fair kicking with not getting his contract renewed and being at a loose end. Willie was great too. He's been kicked up and down the road many times in his life so he can offer a lot of advice. He couldn't believe that I had been dropped, which was encouraging to hear. It's good to have someone with that kind of belief behind you. Then I get this unbelievable stroke of good luck. I think Donncha got the knock about 25 minutes in against Wales. He played on a bit but you could see he was struggling. You could see how gutted he was too. This was supposed to be his day.'

Three years earlier, O'Kelly's career had been revived in similarly fortunate circumstances. Coming off the back of a dispiriting Lions tour, he was dropped for a lacklustre performance in Edinburgh, allowing Gary Longwell in for his first test start in Cardiff. Longwell didn't even last one training session. A broken finger allowed O'Kelly back in, crestfallen but with a point to prove. He'd proved it against Wales and especially against England at Lansdowne Road, where Ireland spoiled a Grand Slam party. He was about to pull the same stunt again. While O'Kelly is one of Ireland's greatest servants, there is no doubt he benefits from the odd adrenaline jolt, the sort that you get from being dropped. It makes him capable of performances that make you wonder how anyone could even consider dropping him in the first place. Twickenham would be a case in point.

Eddie O'Sullivan admits he had a good feeling when they arrived at Twickenham an hour and a half before kickoff on Saturday, 6 March. The squad had been based at the St Anne's Hilton in Wokingham, near Ascot, for Wednesday and Thursday, and training at Bracknell RFC had gone well. The Cheltenham Festival had provided some with a welcome diversion. With their strong racing connections, Guy and Simon Easterby had been pestered for tips. 'I just felt all week that it was coming together nicely,' said O'Sullivan. 'Now, I was never going to say that, of course. It would be suicide to draw that kind of attention. But by the time we got into London, the guys were in the right frame of mind. There was just the right balance between being tense and yet relaxed at the same time. That's often hard to find but it was there.'

Another positive sign was the choice of referee. New Zealander Paul

Honiss had refereed Ireland on six previous occasions and, remarkably, they had won all six – including England at Lansdowne Road in 2001 and France in Paris the year before that. Yet for the Irish hacks drifting into the media centre in the East Stand a couple of hours before kickoff, the feeling was more of trepidation. Twickenham has a special atmosphere but it's not a good place to work. The press box is cramped and exposed with no easy access to the post-match interview area on the far side of the stadium. We also associate it mainly with heavy Irish defeats. In 2002, Ireland had lost 45–11. Two years before that, it was 50–18. Then you had the British hacks. Either they were ramming it down your throat, or they were too embarrassed to make eye contact. It's hard to know which was worse.

There had been something close to unanimity in the Irish newspaper previews – England would win but it was reasonable to expect a decent Irish performance, certainly an improvement on the two previous visits. Even the English press was hoping for the same. There was a sense of Six Nations *ennui*. The tournament needed a jolt. Could Ireland provide it?

'Ireland have the personnel to cause mischief but have they got the mental toughness to carry it through?' asked Mick Cleary in *The Daily Telegraph*. 'We have been here before with Ireland teams at Twickenham, arriving with heady reputations yet departing with mangled egos ... England can have a slight dip in their performance across the board and still expect to finish in front. Ireland have to take themselves to the limit. And then beyond ... England hold the trump cards. Time and again over the last 18 months, they have shown themselves to be masters of winning games. They have not always played well but they have always come through. For all their intermittent stutters, they are the highest of achievers.'

Much of the coverage focused on O'Driscoll's prawn-sandwich jibe, or rather Woodward's prickly response to it. *The Telegraph*'s Paul Hayward reckoned the Irish captain had done his team no favours. 'O'Driscoll's characterisation of Twickenham Man as a supine consumer of sport as corporate hospitality will doubtless endear him to those in white among the 75,000 souls heading to the Fort Knox of rugby today. England have not played a serious match on the site of the old market garden since March of last year. Naturally Sir Clive Woodward OBE – who was just plain old Clive 12 months ago – took a bite out of O'Driscoll yesterday and made it sound like Ireland are in the mayonnaise. "I've got nothing to say to Brian O'Driscoll. We do our talking on the pitch. I'm surprised teams haven't learned that about the English. It's just best to keep quiet."'

Early in the afternoon, England easily won the first women's international at Twickenham, beating a brave Irish side 51–10. There was no hint of insurrection in the air, just a heavy shower half an hour before kickoff that contributed to the surprisingly high error-count.

As it turned out, the main match was not a feast of attacking rugby. Ireland did score a sensational try and D'Arcy always looked threatening when he got his mitts on the ball – four line-breaks in a contest such as this was an extraordinary display of evasion skills. Mostly, though, it was about dismantling the world champions. It was about finding the perfect game plan and then implementing it ruthlessly.

THE FIRST QUARTER – ENGLAND 0 IRELAND 3

MALCOLM O'KELLY (on Ireland's first line-out steal, in the first minute): It was a four-man line-out and a basic call. Their triggers are pretty obvious, to be honest. Thompson threw a very flat ball and we got Pauly up well in front of [Steve] Borthwick. They really needed to hit him at the height of his jump. Maybe Borthwick wasn't used to the different movements at the front, maybe Ben Kay wasn't used to being the senior jumper. But if you can't win ball at two ... well, that's their banker. Whenever England got in trouble at the World Cup, they threw to Martin Johnson there. We just wanted to mess up their Plan A and then see what they came up with.

NIALL O'DONOVAN: The hooker's throwing the ball to a spot in the sky that nobody is near. If his jumpers or lifters are a second slow, he gets the blame. It's high pressure and all you hope to do is make it as uncomfortable for him as possible. You want to make him tighten up. Then you could be in business.

Paul O'Connell pinches Steve Thompson's first line-out throw of the game and the first seed of doubt has been planted. Thompson never recovered and was eventually replaced.

RONAN O'GARA (on his first penalty miss): It still comes back to me every now and again. I can picture it perfectly – I'd say the ball hit the top of the left upright maybe five balls down and screwed away left. Maybe I got my non-kicking foot too close to the ball or I didn't give it enough power. Not a great feeling by any means. After that, there's pressure to make sure your next contribution is a positive one, and I think it was. You don't plan for that sort of start but if it happens you can't dwell on it. There's no looking back. To be honest, that's how I feel about the game in general.

MIKE FORD: I remember the first time they tried to maul the ball at us, about nine minutes in. They'd made about 10 metres and the Twickenham crowd were just beginning to warm up when we smashed them back double the distance. It was a real turning point as far as I was concerned, especially after the success they'd had with their maul against us the previous season. It just sent out the message that we were going to fight for every blade of grass on the pitch.

PAUL ACKFORD (*The Sunday Telegraph*): Iain Balshaw loped to defend Ireland's first probing kick and later he lazily booted a clearance straight into touch. His exaggerated casualness is deceptively attractive in attack when he drifts into space on the run, but when it all goes wrong he simply appears diffident.

SHANE BYRNE: Mike Ford had asked me that morning – 'Are you going to be the one that lets Dawson through? Are you going to be the one that comes to me on Monday with an excuse. Just think Dawson all day.' He [Dawson] came through a ruck early in the game and I was waiting for him. It was sweet. I had a few words in his ear too. There was loads of banter all day: 'Keep it coming.' 'Is that all you've got?' 'Any time you want' – that sort of stuff. I knew after 20 minutes of that game that we weren't going to get beaten. Everybody was playing the way we can play. Every time there was a 50/50 ball, there were two of us. And England aren't the world champions by accident, so you need to play like that from start to finish.

LAWRENCE DALLAGLIO: Ireland came to Twickenham with a very simple game plan – to attack us in the line-out and then use Ronan O'Gara's kicking game. They were really highly motivated as I expected them to be. I just felt disappointed that some of my team-mates were not so willing to target Mr O'Driscoll as I was after his rather inflammatory comments beforehand.

MIKE FORD: Rog finally kicked us in front when they dragged – won our maul. Even at 3–0, the thought crossed my mind that we could be the first team ever to nil England at Twickenham. Honestly. After Munch [Byrne] had decked Dawson, I was never, ever worried.

STUART BARNES (*The Daily Telegraph*): The England wings came up as flat as the centres. Such a system makes a kicking fly-half's game easy if the quality and quantity of possession is as forthcoming as it was on Saturday. When the open-side wing stands flat, there is ample space to boom deep kicks without having to drop them on a sixpence or face the threat of counterattack. Ireland made their intentions clear within 15 minutes but the English defensive shape remained unaltered.

THE SECOND QUARTER – ENGLAND 10 IRELAND 12

MIKE FORD (on Peter Stringer's ankle tap): Jason Robinson's one of those players who can make something out of nothing. Ninety percent of the time, Strings busies around behind the defensive line looking for the chip but this time he was actually in the line, which makes it even more extraordinary that he got back to make the tackle. In the previous Six Nations, he didn't miss a tackle – not one, which is phenomenal. I want to see a perfect green wall and, at times in Twickenham, it was a bit frag-mented. At the same time, that was the only line-break we had. We had 94 percent tackles completed.

EDDIE O'SULLIVAN: Ronan put us 6–0 up in the second quarter. That kick was right on the edge of his range and that will throw some kickers, plus you've got the fact that he'd just been creamed by Hill in the tackle. He had the composure not to force the kick, just to trust his swing. You could pick other kicks from the game. There was the one just before half-time that meant we turned around ahead at 12–10; or there was the conversion of the try that gave us a nine-point buffer. But that one really showed his mental strength.

RONAN O'GARA: He [Hill] rubbed my face in the muck for good measure. I had a go at him that night and he said, 'You hardly expected me to do noth-ing.' If he did nothing, you might think he's not bothered by you, but once you get them doing that to you, you know you have them a bit.

EDDIE O'SULLIVAN: Twenty minutes in, I was happy. Ronan was kicking beautifully and the stats show we'd had 75 percent of the territory. There was still no sign of chariots running around the ground, we weren't two scores down and looking at the clock like previous years. Then they whip-wheeled us at the scrum and the ball squirted out. A try for Matt Dawson. From nothing.

PAUL O'CONNELL: We were all over them yet we were losing. A freaky try off a messy scrum and a penalty and we were a point down. Big deal. We let out a bit of an ol' f*** but we got over it. A bit of mental strength was called for. Like, you're going to be a loser all your life if you throw in the towel every time you let in a soft try. We did an England after that. We ground out a couple of scores.

REGGIE CORRIGAN: I thought our attitude was good after we had con-ceded a soft try. We were as together as we'd ever been. It was a case of 'Lads, we are not accepting this today. We are not lying down.' Then what happens. Scrum to England and the thing comes down on my side. I backed away feeling a little shell shocked, I'll admit.

RONAN O'GARA: The penalty that made it 6–0 was a nice one but the two before the end of the half were even more important, especially for the pack. They set up the two shots at goal and they deserved a reward for the great 40 they'd put in. They deserved to leave the field with a bounce in their step.

HALF-TIME

CLIVE WOODWARD: We'd had some pretty interesting half-time talks at the World Cup. We were 10–3 down against Wales and we hadn't played well in the first half against Samoa. So half-time was good. We were pretty cool, calm and calculated. We had one or two inexperienced players there so it was a case of just calming them down, and just saying, 'This is fine. This happens. We're going to be OK. Let's not change the game plan.' I was concerned about the line-out. You can't win unless you win your line-out. I didn't put it down to the throwing, more just bad calls and some bad execution. So we spoke about it. I think half-time is pretty important in rugby union and I think we got it right against the Irish. We just didn't win the game.

EDDIE O'SULLIVAN: I remember saying at half-time, we're going to win this game if we just keep doing what we're doing, just keep defending as we are, just keep making good decisions. The only change we'd make is that we'd test the outside channels a bit more, keep the ball in hand a bit more. That was the only tactical switch.

THE THIRD QUARTER – ENGLAND 10 IRELAND 19

GORDON D'ARCY (on Ben Cohen's disallowed try): It was catch-22. I was really aware that he was going to step me on the inside but, if I slowed down, I was going to miss him on the inside. He did step. I just threw myself and held on for dear life. If Strings wasn't there to check him, he could have just stretched his hand out and scored. He just nudged him enough to cause a double movement.

STUART BARNES: Balshaw failed to hold Gordon D'Arcy either with his running line or the timing of his pass. People have questioned why Ben Cohen, fast and powerful and a few paces from the line, did not sprint for the corner. The real question is why a left wing was holding the ball under the right arm. If he'd held it under the left arm, he could have used the right arm to fend off D'Arcy. It was a schoolboy error.

NIGEL WILLIAMS (touch judge): The ref glanced at me and I glanced at him and indicated we should go upstairs to Hugh Watkins, the TMO [television match official]. In the meantime, we talked a little and our gut feeling was that it was a try. The IRB's elite referee manager supported the TMO's decision but it was a topic for much discussion later on, I must say, with a fair split in opinion. I still have it on my computer to this day and I still look at it. My point is, if Ben Cohen had placed the ball backwards, as in making the ball available, would he have been penalised for doing so? I've yet to find a referee who would have penalised him. What's the difference between placing it forwards and backwards. There is none. I'm sure it will be much debated in years to come whenever it's shown on television.

MERVYN MURPHY (video analyst, on Girvan Dempsey's try): We knew we could get down their right side because Josh Lewsey shoots up in defence, while Iain Balshaw doesn't close the space quickly enough. There was a little chink there and that's where we went after them.

GORDON D'ARCY: We'd actually called a double miss, so I was meant to be hitting T-Bone [Tyrone Howe] out wide but I stood too deep off Rog and ended up getting it stationary. I took it two steps and whatever way Greenwood angled his shoulder, I just said, 'F*** this, I'm going.' Eddie's attitude

Girvan Dempsey, the ultimate team player, crosses for what Brian O'Driscoll describes as the ultimate team try. Unfortunately for Dempsey, Ben Cohen's sliding studs would force him to retire minutes later.

Billy Whizz (aka Jason Robinson) grabs D'Arcy the Dasher. In a game where defence triumphed over attack, D'Arcy somehow managed to break England's tackle-line on four occasions.

is: If it's on, it's on, but you'd better back yourself. I went for it and after that the pattern just fell into place.

ANTHONY FOLEY: It was straight off the training ground actually, including the sequence of passes running towards the right corner. For a couple of seconds I thought I might pump the legs and get in at the right corner myself. But I think I probably needed Ginger McLoughlin behind me to get me over the line.

EDDIE O'SULLIVAN: We'd worked on that sequence for a long time. The key was O'Driscoll's long pass to T-Bone. If he'd made it immediately like

999 players out of 1,000, Girvan would have been tackled into touch in the corner. But he took two strides to the line and fixed Robinson, who fixed someone else, who fixed Lewsey. He had the ability to read that and execute it under pressure. Then Rog's conversion was crucial as it gave us a nine-point buffer.

BRIAN O'DRISCOLL: I never had any qualms with how Girv was playing, irrespective of what the media was saying. In hindsight, it's great to see that he was the one to score that try. Having said that, if ever there was a team try, this was it.

THE FINAL QUARTER – ENGLAND 13 IRELAND 19

REGGIE CORRIGAN (on O'Kelly's corner tackle): I was right behind [Mark] Regan when he bolted, so I could see the open path for the line in front of him. I thought it was a certain try and, if I thought it, you can bet your life Regan thought it too.

MALCOLM O'KELLY: I knew there was nobody protecting the front of our line-out so when Lawrence Dallaglio came around the outside it was obvious they were going to work a fast one. I made a dash for the corner and hit him [Mark Regan] as hard as I could. I knew he was out. I saw him getting up and doing his jump for joy and I thought: Mark, that might fool the ref, it might fool the touch judge and it might scare the living daylights out of my team-mates, but there's a fella up in the stand somewhere who's going to watch the replay and a dance ain't going to fool him.

PAUL O'CONNELL: What I liked was what was said while we waited for the video ref decisions. We'd be in a huddle and Gleeso [Keith Gleeson] or Axl [Anthony Foley] would be saying, If it's a try, we're going to do x, y or z. We weren't there praying for a decision to go our way. We were just ready to get on with it.

MIKE FORD: We were all waiting for England to crank it up and they started in the last 20. Twice they went to 10 phases but, you know, I don't think they gained any yards.

MALCOLM O'KELLY: England were strong in the last 20, very strong. They got a penalty and [Paul] Grayson knocked it over, then they got another [with three and a half minutes remaining] and they put it into touch. That was a mistake. If they'd got to within three points then the pressure on us would have been even greater.

SIMON EASTERBY: We're fortunate now with the countdown clock, instead of having 10 or 12 minutes of overtime when nobody knew where they stood. It had just turned 40 and I was just desperate for someone to boot it off the park.

GORDON D'ARCY: I was calling for that ball before Stringer decided to bounce around with it. I couldn't believe it. I just wanted it kicked high into the stand. If it's in the stand, they can't take a quick throw. If there's more time to be played, we can get a little injury, we can get our defence organised. As it turned out it was the last kick. Unbelievable.

*   *   *

AT some time that evening, Eddie O'Sullivan must have clenched his fists, punched the air and let out a triumphant yelp. England. Twickenham. Yessss. When it happened, it was behind closed doors. In public, the coach was keeping his game face on. We saw it when Girvan Dempsey scored. O'Sullivan must have sensed the cameras of the world would zoom in for a reaction shot. After a couple of claps, he buttoned his blazer, folded his arms and crossed his legs. In five seconds, there was enough material for an entire Desmond Morris seminar. O'Sullivan later explained he was merely trying to concentrate on what happened next. He was no use to anyone doing a jig. It was about getting a radio message down to Mervyn Murphy on the touchline. 'Focus on the restart. Get it right. Don't blow it now.'

While the final whistle may have signalled the end of work for the players, their coach still had business to attend to. Like getting his players off the field for starters. Some, like Reggie Corrigan and John Hayes, were almost too tired to move – the eight forwards had played the entire 80 minutes, remember. Others wanted to savour the moment, to acknowledge the

After four and a half years of impregnability, Fortress Twickenham is no more. Kevin Maggs, Gordon D'Arcy and Keith Gleeson celebrate, while Lawrence Dallaglio looks dazed.

groups of delirious green-clad supporters. What about the Millennium Trophy, some of them wondered (the custom is to present it at the post-match dinner, incidentally). One player admitted he was happy to keep the English players standing a little longer at the entrance to the tunnel, where they were waiting to clap the winners in. But soon O'Sullivan was amongst them, shepherding them in that direction. Let's not milk this. Let's be dignified.

Clive Woodward was dignified too. Ten minutes after they had returned to the dressing room, he was in to congratulate the Irish players and wish them well for the remainder of the championship that had just been blown wide open.

'I'm very clear on that,' Woodward said a couple of months later. 'Whenever I lose, I make a point of going into the opposition changing room. It wasn't easy. You haven't lost a game in four and a half years at Twickenham. It's not easy, especially when your team doesn't play well. That said, we didn't prepare well and we got what we deserved. I think history will look back on that as a game we were meant to lose and it will do us good to have lost it. I think we'll see in a year's time. England will be right when we play at Lansdowne Road next year.

'I wasn't confident going into the game, not at all. For one thing, I've got a lot of respect for the Irish team, for the players and their coach. Then there was the stage we were at. We went into the World Cup as probably the best-prepared team and, despite not playing well, we won the damn thing. I think we went into the Six Nations as probably the worst-prepared team and we just couldn't get the whole thing back together. You know, missing guys like Johnson and Wilkinson, bringing in a new guy at ten who had only just started working for you. You saw a very experienced Irish team and said this is going to be a very close game. You just knew we weren't prepared properly and the Irish were. They deserved to win, as I keep telling everyone.'

O'Sullivan appreciated the gesture. Five years previously he had been in the same changing room with a US Eagles team that that just lost 114–0. Woodward came in then to console, reminding the visitors that only a year previously England had been beaten 76–0 in Australia. A year, he advised them, was a long time in rugby 'He didn't have to do that,' said O'Sullivan, 'just as he didn't have to come in to congratulate us. I'd be biased because I get on well with Clive, but the thing I liked was that he said the same thing publicly as he said privately. There was no spin, no complaints. We were the better team, fair and square.'

As soon as his media duties were over, O'Sullivan switched on his mobile phone and there was a message of congratulations from Jack Clark, the managing director of US Rugby, and Tom Billups, the Eagles' coach. There were a million other messages too. 'My phone went bananas,' said O'Sullivan. 'It was mayhem out in the Twickenham car park too. There were so many supporters there that it took an age to get everyone on the bus and on the road.'

If only the evening had gone as much to plan as the game. The English Rugby Union don't provide police escorts from Twickenham, only to the stadium and, even then, the driver stops at every traffic light ('Give me the gardaí any day,' said John Redmond, 'or the Italians. Their outriders are actually scary.'). Heavy London traffic meant it took an hour and a half to get back to The Chelsea Harbour Hotel. There weren't too many complaints. Guy Easterby was his usual entertaining self on the microphone, coaxing a few songs out of Anthony Foley, who had won his fiftieth cap that day – not a bad occasion to do so. Other players got a chance to sit and chat with wives and girlfriends.'

The sense of having spoilt the homecoming celebrations was only accentuated by the fact that the Irish party finally made it to the banquet at the Intercontinental Hotel an hour late. 'I think when we walked into the dinner was the best moment,' said Corrigan. 'There were about 700 people at this dinner and it was set up very much as a World Cup celebration. You had the Webb Ellis Trophy here, a string quartet there, a brass section over in this corner. We arrived in, we suddenly noticed it went a bit quieter, the music lowered. You could see all these old lads sitting around sipping glasses of wine. You knew you hadn't just spoiled the party, you'd absolutely ruined it. Maggsy was hilarious. He was straight up to this bar in the middle of the room, ordering beers all round in his loudest voice. He was really rubbing it in – he was loving it obviously. You just sat down and looked around. They were very quiet. It had hit home.'

Like Maggs, Mike Ford just had to rub it in. When he bumped into Jason Robinson, he couldn't stop himself from asking Robinson where did he think Ireland's attacking threat would come from. All light-hearted stuff. There was more banter with Phil Larder, one of Ford's former coaches. 'It's good to lose every now and again,' said Ford. 'You should know,' responded Larder.

The meal and speeches didn't end until 12.30 and the players got separated after that. London can have that effect. Malcolm O'Kelly remembers trying to get into a nightclub with Ronan O'Gara and their girlfriends but being refused entry. Anthony Foley had to hide in a cupboard from people who were trying to ply him with drink – he phoned Keith Wood from his hiding place to see if they could meet for a quiet jar. Corrigan, Shane Byrne and Victor Costello ended up leading a singsong in The Morrison, a pub on the King's Road owned by two Irishmen, Stephen Breen and Eoin Brophy. Then they went hobnobbing with the glitterati.

'We met Patrick Kielty and he brought us back to his place for a beer,' said Corrigan. 'We were all just chilling out. He was telling us how he'd just got the deal to present *Who Wants to be a Millionaire?* over in LA. Dallaglio arrived at about 2.00 with his missus. Jodie Kidd was there – I have to say it was a pretty cool way to end the night, talking to Jodie Kidd about cars. Of course, I had to do the typical Paddy thing. I was straight over with the picture phone, putting my arm around her so I could email everyone when I got home.' Look at me, ma. Top of the world.

CHAPTER 5 – ITALY & SCOTLAND

CLOSING THE DEAL

England had not lost a championship game at Twickenham since 1997 so the postmortem carried out in the Monday papers was grim. 'No Jonno, no Wilko and it all falls apart for England' was how former England out-half Rob Andrew put it in *The Daily Mail*. Chris Hewett in the London *Independent* described it thus: 'England were obliterated at the line-out, marmalised in the tackle and smithereened in the battle for possession. The only things the world champions did not lose were the error count – which they won all too easily – and the shirts of their backs. The Irish, profoundly unimpressed by their opponents' skintight fashionwear, did not want them anyway.'

There were harsh words from upstairs at Twickenham too. Fran Cotton, the chairman of the English RFU's Club England Committee, blamed the defeat on the distraction caused by financial squabbles over player image rights. 'You do not want to be in meetings during the week you are preparing for a test match,' Cotton told the *Mail*. 'Nor do you want players going into hospitality events at their hotel. They have been pulled from pillar to post since the World Cup but they have to realise what got them there in the first place – total concentration on the job.'

There was little chance that the Irish players would now be allowed to lose concentration. On Sunday evening, some of them ventured out for a celebratory pint in Dublin's city centre, where they encountered plenty of back-slapping bonhomie. 'We were being treated more like soccer stars,' recalled Malcolm O'Kelly. 'It didn't really sit well with me, to be honest. I'd be more able to handle the abuse than the back-slapping. We didn't make a meal of it. And, anyway, when you turn up for training on Tuesday morning and Eddie's there with his hands on his hips, you know it's time to move on.'

Ireland had been promoted to fifth in the world rankings. The newspapers were awash with Triple Crown talk. On top of that, Ireland had spoiled the tournament organisers' plans for a Grand Slam *finale* in Paris on Saturday, 27 March. All going well, they even had an outside chance of winning the championship. Points difference was against them – they stood at plus nine, whereas England were plus 57, France plus 60. If, however, they could rack up big wins against Italy and Scotland and if England could win narrowly in Paris, it was still on. If, if.

O'Sullivan took out his fire extinguisher and doused it all down. He'd been here before. The previous season, Ireland won their first three championship games and suddenly everything was being geared towards a Grand Slam showdown against England in Dublin. The intervening trip to Cardiff was written off as irrelevant. As it turned out, Ireland only scraped home 18–16 courtesy of a wobbly injury-time drop-goal from Ronan O'Gara. This time there would be no distractions. Triple Crown talk – and talk of winning the tournament – was banned. Ireland had to beat Italy. The scoreline was irrelevant too. 'Things can change very quickly in this game. There's only six inches between a pat on the back and a kick in the arse,' said O'Sullivan in typical O'Sullivan fashion.

So he chucked us hacks another story to keep us occupied. Geordan Murphy was back. So too was Mike McGurn, incidentally – evidently, he had sorted out his problems with the IRFU. Murphy was a bigger story, though. The previous year he had been the star of Ireland's championship. He was set for a big World Cup but fractured his tibia and fibula in a freak fall playing against Scotland just 24 hours before the squad was due to be announced. Now, six months later, after just three games for Leicester, he was back.

Murphy replaced Tyrone Howe on the wing, meaning that, for the first time in the history of the championship, Ireland would start a game without an Ulstermen in the side. So much for those quota theories. The selection was a little harsh on Howe, who had a storming game at Twickenham, showing characteristic grit in the final minutes when he scrambled his team to safety on the dead-ball line. On the other hand, it also meant Ireland could field a truly sexy three-quarter line against the Italians: Murphy, D'Arcy, O'Driscoll and Horgan. O'Sullivan may have dismissed any talk of racking up points against the *azzurri* but you could still fantasise.

The dream was swept aside by a demonic wind that came whipping in off Dublin Bay on the morning of the game. Ireland had trained in sleet on the Thursday and when they turned up at Lansdowne Road on Saturday, a gale was flattening the touch flags and tossing tackle bags about like tumbleweed. There could have been no more obvious reminder that Ireland were playing their home games in an embarrassingly antiquated stadium. It was impossible to predict the flight of the ball and Ronan O'Gara, often resembling the hapless parent chasing his unruly brat, found the experience highly frustrating.

'The games against Wales and Italy were farcical, to be honest,' he said. 'Professionals shouldn't have to play in those conditions. No-one should. I don't know if I'll still be in the team when Lansdowne Road is redeveloped but it can't happen soon enough. With first-class stadiums, the wind doesn't really affect the flight of the ball. But for those games, it was impossible. You're looking forward to it all week and then you don't get the chance to show what you're capable of.'

It didn't help Ireland's cause that they persisted with plans for a wide game during a gale-assisted first half. The more they tried, the more the ball ended up on the floor and the more frustrated the players looked. With half-time approaching, it took two pieces of opportunism to steady things. O'Driscoll showed great awareness and stunning pace to whiz past the blind-side cover and score his twenty-fourth try for Ireland, breaking Denis Hickie's record in the process.

Meanwhile Malcolm O'Kelly was equalling Bill McBride's record of 63 caps, the most for an Irish lock. With Paul O'Connell missing because of bruised ribs, O'Kelly was called upon to provide plenty of McBride-like grunt. He also did things that McBride would never have dreamed of even attempting – running a decoy line for O'Driscoll's try, or intercepting a quick throw at the front of the line-out to score. He was everywhere. Having made a point at Twickenham, here was evidence that he intended to keep on making that point.

'From the time that he came back in, Malcolm focused extremely well,' said O'Sullivan. 'I'd a long, hard discussion when I dropped him and another long, hard discussion when I picked him. Originally, I felt he wasn't delivering to the level he needed to get to. When he did turn the corner, it was like, well, what are you going to do to stay there? He had to make sure he didn't lapse back to where he was, which can happen to anyone. It's easy to focus when things are going badly. It's harder to focus when things are going well. But he just got his head together and had an outstanding championship. From the time he got back in, his games were outstanding, right up there with Paul O'Connell's.'

Shane Horgan's try early in the second half made the game virtually safe at 19–0 but there was still a lot of spadework needed to protect that lead. The conditions favoured the Italians, who like nothing better than to bash away at the fringes, playing brutal, attritional rugby. Shane Byrne reckoned that, physically, it was the most punishing game he had ever played. He wasn't alone.

'We knew it was going to be a tackle-fest and it was,' says Gordon D'Arcy. 'The Italians kept coming and coming and coming. They were cheap-shotting, in your face, elbowing you, doing whatever they wanted. You couldn't say it was a whole load of fun.'

Ireland lost O'Driscoll to the sin bin for a high tackle on Italian scrumhalf Paul Griffen. Yet all they conceded in terms of points was a solitary penalty to Roland de Marigny. O'Sullivan could afford to be happy with a professional performance. 'Italy was a big challenge for a couple of reasons,' he said. 'Traditionally, Ireland would have beaten England and then underperformed against Italy. We had to put England out of our minds and keep the Triple Crown out of our minds too. We had to push in two directions mentally – and then we had to deal with the weather. It was after the Italian match that we achieved all three things. We hadn't hammered Italy but we were never going to hammer Italy in those conditions. That sort of experience stands you in good stead. You learn how to deal with the here and now.'

*　*　*

There were casualties of the trench warfare, though. Keith Gleeson went off in the sixty-fourth minute with a broken arm that ended his season. John Hayes's back went into spasm after the game and for a while he was looking very doubtful for the Scotland game. Neither Reggie Corrigan nor Frankie Sheahan were 100 percent and when Marcus Horan, the reserve prop, hurt his shoulder in training the following Monday, there was suddenly a front-row crisis. Munster's Frankie Roche was called in and briefly it looked like more reinforcements might be needed – if they could be found.

It didn't take long for word to get to Matt Williams, the Scotland coach. The Australian had been in charge at Leinster the previous season, and had kept in touch with a couple of his former charges. Reggie Corrigan received a congratulatory text message after the win in Twickenham, to which he replied: *Thanks very much, buddy. Don't think you're coming back to wreck the party.* Williams responded: *And don't think we're coming over to make up the numbers.* By coincidence, Williams bumped into Frieda Corrigan on the Thursday evening before the game. Wives and girlfriends of the Irish players were having a pre-dinner drink in The Waterloo pub on Pembroke Road, when the Scotland coach just happened along. Try though he might, he couldn't extract any information on the physical condition of Ireland's tight forwards.

Williams needed all the help he could get. Just as Ireland were chasing their first Triple Crown since 1985, it had been 19 years since Scotland had suffered the ignominy of a championship whitewash. Williams was only four games in to his reign as Scotland coach but his honeymoon period was long over. He had asked for patience, but patience was wearing thin after a clueless, passionless performance in Rome, where Scotland lost 20–14. And while the coach was blaming referees, former Scottish internationals were blaming him. On the day of the Ireland match, David Sole wrote in *The Daily Telegraph*: 'Scotland should offer no great resistance and it should be a formality. Normally I would hold out some faint hope that the Scots could produce an upset as they have the capability to show character and fight, which often makes up for ability or nous. But this year, even I cannot see much evidence of this based on recent performances.'

As for Ireland, by this stage O'Sullivan's Triple Crown embargo had been fully lifted. There was just no escaping it. The media began wheeling out the 1985 veterans for inspection. The demand for tickets was enormous. O'Kelly, a regular visitor to Old Trafford, had even been asked to arrange a couple for Bert Beckham, father of you-know-who. The Citywest Hotel, which had seemed like a hideaway in no-man's land, was now buzzing with autograph hunters. The players had never signed so many shirts and photographs in one week and couldn't help getting the feeling that certain people were looking to cash in on their success.

Not that they were taking success against Scotland for granted. Kevin Maggs, a survivor from the bad old days when Ireland lost more games than they won, spent the week urging team-mates to seize the opportunity, not to freeze on the big occasion. Brian O'Driscoll, about to win his fiftieth cap, was pushing the same attitude. 'It was great that Drico was captain,' said Paul O'Connell, who had recovered in time to play. 'He thrives on added pressure. He said there'd be questions asked about whether we could handle the pressure of expectation. He loved having that pressure. He said, "This is where we want to be, playing for Triple Crowns." The more you hear that kind of stuff, the more you see someone in that frame of mind, the more you believe it.'

Yet somehow it was inevitable that the sense of occasion would have a levelling effect. Scotland had nothing to lose; Ireland had everything. It showed within 30 seconds of kickoff. A nervous-looking O'Gara had his first punt blocked by Chris Cusiter, leading indirectly to a Scotland penalty by Chris Paterson. It would take O'Gara half the game to recover his composure. It didn't help his cause that he was playing behind a far from rampant pack. Ireland's line-out had been formidable but, in Scott Murray, Williams had a roaming jumper who could upset any system. The Scots also borrowed heavily from the back-catalogue of Ireland v Scotland games, spoiling and mullocking wherever possible.

At times they were plain nasty, clearly targeting Brian O'Driscoll for some rough stuff. Early on, he was the recipient of a high, stiff arm from Tom Philip. Later in the first half, he felt Simon Webster's studs down the back of his head. 'I was disappointed by that,' O'Sullivan later said. 'There were two nasty incidents which left a sour taste in everybody's mouth. Certainly, the standing on the head ... put it this way, I was surprised Webster got away with it. I mean, he nearly took Brian's head off. I don't associate that sort of behaviour with Scottish rugby. We've often had ding-dongs but you never got that sort of stuff.'

Mercifully, the conditions were relatively mild, enablng Ireland to put some width on the ball. A sublime miss pass by O'Driscoll set up D'Arcy for his first test try – which seemed a remarkable statistic, given the championship he had been through. Then, two minutes before half-time, another long O'Driscoll pass sent Murphy over to the left corner. Two tries from seven set-piece possessions in the first half was a decent strike rate. It was still a ball-game, though. The Scottish pack had set up a second penalty for Paterson, while out-half Dan Parks had landed a long-range drop-goal, making it 16–9 at the break. Then things got interesting. A bit too interesting.

The first five minutes of the second half could have been cut from any Scotland v Ireland game of the 1990s, when Scotland never lost. Watching the visitors punching away close in and rucking like demons, you half-expected Jim Telfer to materialise in a tracksuit, cracking the whip and roaring 'Get lower!' Sure enough, after the ball had been recycled relentlessly through 13 phases, Allister Hogg spied a gap at the side of a ruck and plunged over. The score line was 16–16. Game on.

Geordan Murphy flies past Simon Danielli for Ireland's second try against Scotland. The Irish backs looked like causing havoc – whenever they could get their hands on the ball.

'I have to admit, the first thing that came into my mind was S***, are we going to blow this?' said Corrigan. 'The Scots weren't lying down the way we secretly expected them to. That said, I don't think it was complacency on our part. We just hadn't been as sharp as usual and in that 40 to 50 minutes, they'd played their best rugby for the season. I never really doubted that we were going to win the game. There was just a sense of "Can we get on with it, please?"'

Ireland did just that. O'Gara set up an attacking line-out in the Wanderers' clubhouse corner. There was a growing sense of communal desperation as first O'Connell and then Foley lunged for the line, a sense also that the Scots would get a huge psychological lift if they could survive this assault. Ireland had actually lost a metre or two of ground when Peter Stringer passed to David Wallace, standing to the left of the ruck, with the blue

Scottish flanker Allister Hogg burrows over early in the second half to make it 16–16. Hadn't the Scots read the script?

defensive wall ahead of him. As O'Driscoll had done in the first half against Wales, he made something out of nothing, spinning out of Parks's tackle and then crashing through three or four more bodies to score. Cue pandemonium.

'Only Wally could have scored that try,' said O'Sullivan. 'Only he could get a ball and climb out of three tackles. He's an incredibly powerful man. David Wallace could play as a running back in the NFL, he's so quick and strong. You put him through the tiniest of gaps with some blockers and he'd run over somebody and get first down every time. Only he could do that, and we needed him to do that at that point. We'd dug ourselves into a bit of a hole there. At the same time, when they were in the huddle under the posts, the fellas knew all they had to do here was get a field position, stay there and get a score, be it a penalty, a drop-goal or whatever. They knew that if we kept them under pressure for long enough they'd give up a score. I didn't have to send that message in. There were enough senior players to figure out what's important.'

There were still 27 minutes remaining, but the Scots had nothing more to give. With a keen sense of dramatic timing, D'Arcy moved centre stage again. A barnstorming run up the middle set up the scrum which, in turn, became the ruck from which Stringer sealed the results. Then came a delicious one-two with Murphy to set up his second try, a fitting note to end his phenomenal championship.

'I actually preferred the first try because it was my first for Ireland,' D'Arcy said later. 'It was funny. A couple of my mates made a few bob out of it. They'd been betting on me to be first try-scorer in every game. My odds starting getting longer and longer as the tournament went on so they made their money back right at the end. It was a move we knew could work and Drico threw out a lovely ball. As for the second one, I called a switch with Rog but there were four Scottish lads in front of me, so I said "Screw this", stepped sideways, looked up and, Hallelujah, there was a massive gap. It was easy from there.'

As O'Sullivan emptied his substitutes' bench, the carnival atmosphere at Lansdowne Road began to build. And when, at precisely 5:41pm, David Humphreys hoofed the ball into the East Stand, it was the signal for a prolonged and oddly moving celebration. That day, in his *Irish Times* column, former international Donal Spring questioned the relevance of the Triple Crown in the modern professional age. Yet for the majority of the Lansdowne crowd, who deferred the customary post-match rush to the pub, it clearly *was* still relevant.

The lap of honour was an expression of relief as much as anything else. As O'Sullivan pointed out, the achievement was sweeter for having been made to work harder than expected by the Scots. 'I'd been saying all week that Scotland would play well and I genuinely believed they would. They'd had four poor performances in the championship up to that point. There was always going to be one big performance in them. And Scotland are like us. They love coming to town to spoil a party.

'The big test for me that week was to convince the players that this was going to be no garden party, that if we got it wrong we'd lose. They could beat us. The fact that we had that approach all week was crucial when they equalised the game in the second half. Here we are 16–16, do you want it or don't you? It was just as well that we had discussed this possibility. If we hadn't, there might have been panic and that wasn't a gamble I wanted to take. So the key was to get rid of all this nonsense about how we were going to hockey them or about how we might still win the championship on points difference.

'As for the lap of honour, you don't plan for stuff like that. After the Twickenham game, I was very cognisant that players were elated but I wanted to get everyone off the field. Good job, well done, game over, now let's get into the changing room. And in some ways I felt the same after Scotland. But the crowd actually stayed in the stadium. There was this massive response from them, and all these green flags. Someone started heading down the touchline and it took off from there. It was a fairly bedraggled lap of honour but the crowd appreciated it and that's why you do the lap. It's in their honour, really.'

*　　*　　*

And so, 19 years after he had been whisked away to Heuston Station at a critical moment, Ronan O'Gara finally got to enjoy a Triple Crown celebration. A couple of days before the game, he had received a text message from Donal Lenihan, the man who had set up Michael Kiernan's famous drop-goal against England: *At least I'll do you the courtesy of staying until the final whistle this time around.* With the score at 16–16, the thought occurred that O'Gara might have been called ashore, because, at that stage, he was having a poor game by his standards. It wasn't a thought that crossed his mind, he says. In the end, he wasn't replaced until the final minutes, by which stage he had recovered his composure. It was a more appropriate end to what had been, personally speaking, a fine championship.

As for his mum and dad, their first port of call was the IRFU's hospitality

The team photo, like the lap of honour, was short on planning, high on emotion. Shane Byrne's Scottish jersey was airbrushed out in most of the commemorative posters.

area under the West Stand, where the players' parents congregate for a post-match cup of tea. Fergal O'Gara was prepared for more ribbing about 'staying the distance' – the story of his early exit in 1985 had got around at this stage. As he entered the hospitality area, he sensed something was wrong. People were clustered in small groups, speaking in hushed tones. It was then that he heard the tragic news about John McCall.

Only a few hours previously, the 19-year-old from Armagh had run out at King's Park, Durban, to play for Ireland in their under-19 World Championship opener against New Zealand. Twenty minutes into the game, he was doing what he did best, trying to win a ball on the ground. But when the ruck broke up, McCall lay motionless on the turf. He was stretchered from the field by paramedics and rushed to the King's Park Medical Centre.

The Irish squad had only been in South Africa a few days but already the red-headed flanker had established himself as a character, a livewire. A leader, too. Just 10 days previously, he had captained the Royal School, Armagh, to victory in the final of the Ulster Schools Senior Cup at Ravenhill. He came from a well-known rugby family. Brian, his uncle, was capped for Ireland and indeed made an appearance as a substitute against France in 1985, the year John was born. His dad, Ian, still plays junior rugby for Armagh.

As the game continued at King's Park, it became clear that John McCall was battling for his life. Michael Cunningham, the team manager, was told by the doctor on duty at the medical centre that he should contact the boy's parents as soon as possible.

This took longer than expected. Cunningham's contact number for Ian McCall kept ringing out so he called Joan Breslin, the IRFU's Squads Administrator, who would have backup numbers. No luck. By the time the news got to Philip Browne, the union's chief executive, it was half an hour before kickoff at Lansdowne Road. By then, McCall's death had been confirmed. It would later emerge that he had suffered cardiac arrest arising from swollen heart muscles – in other words, sudden death syndrome. While only a few people knew it, what had been planned as one of Irish rugby's happiest days was already one of its saddest.

Browne and Martin Murphy, the union's operations director, headed back to 62 Lansdowne Road and switched the rugby network into alert mode. They rang Barry O'Driscoll, a member of the IRB's medical committee and asked him to contact his South African counterpart with a view to providing whatever help was possible. It emerged that the Irish group were staying in the same Durban hotel as the Australian squad, who came equipped with a sports psychologist who specialised in trauma. He would provide counselling for management and players. John Callaghan, a member of the IRFU committee, was enlisted to contact members of Armagh RFC in order set up a local support system for the McCall family.

Contacting the McCall family had proved difficult, however. A message was sent out several times over the Lansdowne Road PA system just in case they were present at the game. It was during the half-time interval that Browne finally got Ian McCall on his mobile phone. He had been watching the Scotland game on television at home. Only then could he pass on the terrible news.

There were about 10 minutes remaining when Browne and Murphy made it back to the stadium. By then, John Redmond had drafted an official IRFU statement, expressing sympathy to the McCall family, their friends and everyone involved with the under-19 squad. The news spread quickly. Eddie O'Sullivan was taken aside just after he had finished his post-match television interview. By the time he got down to the dressing room, the players had heard. Bottles of champagne were left unopened. There would be a minute's silence before that evening's banquet.

'It was just such a shock,' O'Driscoll said later. 'One minute you're doing a television interview about how great it is to win a Triple Crown, the next you're there trying to come to terms with news like this. Because rugby's such a tightknit community, everyone's thoughts were very much with family and friends. My cousin Cillian Willis was the Ireland scrum-half in that game in Durban. I'd taken part in an under-19 championship a few years earlier. It put everything in perspective. You could say our celebrations were deferred for a day or so.'

According to those close to the family, the McCalls – Ian, Carolyn, Rebecca and James – showed remarkable courage through a harrowing experience. Within 24 hours, Ian travelled out to South Africa with a friend to bring his son's body home. At the family wake, they played the video of the match in Durban over and over. There was no better way to remember John than to see him do what he most loved doing. The family was touched by the decision of the Natal RFU to name the medical centre at King's Park after their son and they have been overwhelmed by the compassion shown by the general rugby community.

As Fergal O'Gara said, the John McCall tragedy is every parent's worst nightmare. O'Gara had just settled in Cork in 1981 when Gus Barrett broke his neck playing a Dudley Cup game for UCC against UCD at The Mardyke. Barrett died a few years later. 'As your kids are growing up, it's always there in the back of your mind, but you can't lead your life like that. If you're a family involved in sport, you wish your kids well and hope everything goes OK but sometimes, in the space of split second, everything flashes in front of you. It was like that on the day of the Triple Crown game. I'd had a slight inclination something was wrong when I head the message repeated over the PA during the game. Then, in the midst of all the celebrations after-wards, you hear the news. I just thought, My God, how the world can be turned on its head in the space of 10 seconds.'

*   *   *

France completed their Grand Slam by beating England 24–21 at the Stade de France later that evening. Much later, in fact – French televi-sion had dictated a bizarre 9.00pm kickoff. We can only imagine Clive Woodward's mood as he sat through after-dinner speeches – in French *and* English – in the small hours of the morning. Within four months, England had gone from best in the world to third in Europe. It didn't get much better for them either. In June, Woodward took a tired and depleted squad to New Zealand and Australia, where they were duly thumped in all three tests.

Things didn't turn quite so sour in Ireland but the season did fizzle out a bit. Munster, the only Irish province to make it to the knockout stages of the European Cup, were stung by Wasps at the end of a thrilling semi-final at Lansdowne Road on the last Sunday in April. Connacht, after another excel-lent run in the Challenge Cup, also suffered a semi-final defeat (to Harle-quins) earlier that day. As for Leinster, they had their traditional end-of-season bitching, with a few players moaning anonymously in the press about Gary Ella, who was fired shortly afterwards. Before returning to Australia, Ella would also use the press to have his own say, complaining bitterly about the lack of professionalism of several senior players.

In June, the Irish squad headed to South Africa under something of a cloud, having threatened to strike over tour fees. They travelled as favour-ites but lost both tests to the Springboks, in Bloemfontein and Cape Town. Questions were raised about the players' mental attitude going into the series and there were rumours of end-of-season disharmony amongst the players. This took some of the gloss off the Triple Crown.

But certain memories are slow to fade. O'Driscoll's glorious two-try comeback against Wales; Shane Byrne's manic celebrations in the same game; Paul O'Connell picking off Steve Thompson's throws at Twicken-ham; Peter Stringer flicking Jason Robinson's ankle; the exquisite approach work for Girvan Dempsey's try; Ronan O'Gara's towering conversion; Malcolm O'Kelly's phenomenal corner-flag tackle on Mark Regan.

Above all, it will be remembered as D'Arcy's year. If 1899 was Louis Magee and 1948 was Jack Kyle and 1982 was Ollie Campbell, then 2004 belonged to Gordon D'Arcy. To excel playing in a new position took every-body – especially the video analysts in Wales and England – completely by surprise. To do so from a state of relative obscurity in January made the story even more magical.

When the *BBC Sport* website conducted a poll for Player of the Six Nations, D'Arcy pulled in a whopping 12,000 votes, which was 50 percent of the ballot (Paul O'Connell was second on 13 percent, Ben Cohen next on 9 percent, followed by Gareth Thomas on 8 percent and Serge Betsen on 6 percent). Typical of his elevated profile, D'Arcy was making a public appearance when he heard the news, presenting a trophy to 10-year-olds at Wexford Wanderers RFC.

There were now lots of people who wanted to be associated with him. BMW wanted him to drive one of their cars. Adidas made him customised boots. The IRFU tried to get him to sign a four-year contract. He wasn't just appearing in the sports pages either. Kevin Myers, the *Irish Times* colum-nist, wanted to know how D'Arcy and O'Driscoll came to be. How, he won-dered, could you have two 5ft 11in, 15-stoners with low centres of gravity and explosive power, born within 12 months of each other? 'What exactly was happening a quarter of a century or so ago? What was going on in the bedrooms of Ireland that people started creating marvellous rugby players? Was there a popular guidebook to sexual practices which encouraged would-be mothers to assume one position which would within a dozen years or so produce a budding centre? We certainly need to know ... For as we all must be aware, the purpose of sex is not pleasure but to knit rugby players out of human wool, which was certainly what was happening between the sheets of Ireland sometime around 1980.'

Various theories were proposed to explain D'Arcy's sudden blossoming, especially in the week that Matt Williams came to Dublin. The most re-heated story was the one about Williams bawling D'Arcy out on the training pitch because there was beer on his breath. Williams had also threatened the player with not renewing his Leinster contract a couple of years previously unless he showed a change in attitude. So the story went anyway. When D'Arcy shredded the Scottish defence at Lansdowne Road, Williams derived a measure of satisfaction. 'I'm delighted the little bugger did that to me today,' Williams said. 'You spend four years working on him and he comes out and does that.'

D'Arcy says too much was made of his relationship with Williams, however. 'People were saying, "Matt Williams resurrected your career." One small thing got blown out of all proportion. I said in one interview that I was acting the bollocks when he arrived and he told me to prove to him I was worth keeping for a contract. It was just like dangling a carrot, there was nothing more to it. I was going to get a contract. It was just a way of saying, Cut your messing and start training hard. I did. But the media got hold of it and Matt joined in.

'Matt had an influence in the rejuvenation of my career and it took three years to get to the stage I was at. But he wasn't the only one. Like, my dad told me, "You're doing this properly, or you're going back to college. I'm not going to let you spend five years messing around and occasionally making the bench for Leinster. Either do it or get the f*** out of it." That was somebody giving you a kick up the ass. I'd just met Fintan Drury [D'Arcy's agent] at that stage too. He told me I had promise but I wasn't delivering. It was bare-faced honesty from people like that which motivated me more than anything else.

'That said, I wouldn't change a thing, not a hope. It's the road less travelled. There are different ways of looking at it. I probably shouldn't have got a cap at 19. If I was to be given the cap, I probably should have been looked after better. Perhaps I needed a more regimented approach. I used to be the kind of guy who, if you let me test the boundaries, I'd test them, whereas now, I set my own boundaries. I have to and that's the reality.'

The same philosophy applied to the 2004 Ireland team. After 1985, when Ireland had won their second outright championship in the space of four years, such was the general sense of self-satisfaction that a talented bunch of players proceeded to underachieve wantonly. The 2004 players were acutely aware that the Triple Crown needed to be the springboard to greater things.

It really hit home with Paul O'Connell at an awards dinner hosted by the Irish Rugby Union Players Association (IRUPA) in April. The guest speaker was former England lock, Martin Bayfield, who was the butt of a hundred jokes, all to do with England's 'ignominious' defeat to Ireland at Twickenham. The jokes soon rang hollow for O'Connell. 'It was good to see all the clips again on the big screen,' he says. 'But it was a pity that the whole point of showing the try at Twickenham seemed to be so that they could slag yer man Bayfield. We should be looking to change that attitude a bit. Everyone gets so excited when we beat England but it shouldn't be such an uncommon occurrence. I enjoyed winning a Triple Crown and I know they'll be peddling pictures of us in years to come. But I couldn't say that it's something I really treasure just yet. I'm sure I will in the future but I hope to win a few more. We haven't come all this way just to be content with that.'

This is essentially the same message O'Connell communicated in his newspaper column the Monday after Ireland had beaten Scotland. It's an attitude echoed by Brian O'Driscoll. 'Captaining Ireland to a Triple Crown means I'm fortunate to join a pretty elite club – there are only four other Irishmen who have done it. To be in with those boys gives me a great sense of satisfaction. But the Triple Crown is done now. You dwell on it for a while and then you move on.'

Such ambition is encouraging. It's the same sort of attitude we saw from the Ireland Under-21 team who got to a World Cup final in Glasgow in June 2004 only to be beaten by an outstanding New Zealand side. Beating France in the semi-final – and thus becoming the first northern hemisphere side to reach the under-19 final – was seen as a step along a path rather than as an end in itself. Increasingly, Irish representative teams take the field aiming to be successful. And, as professionals, Eddie O'Sullivan and his players have no option but to think that way.

In reflective moments, however, they can still look back at the 2004 Triple Crown and purr with satisfaction. Anthony Foley, for example, will now always have something over his childhood friend from Killaloe, Keith Wood. Others have enjoyed the reaction they got from Joe Public, who was still giving thumbs up and honking his car horn in acknowledgement months after that win over Scotland. Maybe it's the historical aspect to the Triple Crown. It's older than everything – the Six Nations, the Five Nations, the World Cup, the Grand Slam. Maybe it's the fact that, up until 2004, Ireland had won just six of them in 103 attempts. It remains to be seen whether this truly was a seminal moment but, either way, it was a special one. A certain group of Irishmen know that they will always be remembered as the 2004 team.

No-one knows it better than Ronan O'Gara, who finally got the perfect end to a 19-year-old yarn. 'This is the first time this bunch of players have won anything and we've been together for a number of years now,' he said. 'All the players are very close and we've had enjoyable times together. In years to come, 10 or 20 years after we've retired, we've always something we can always come back to. Fellas appreciate that. It's nice to be able to see you achieved something with such a good bunch of lads. There will always be that bond.'

APPENDIX – IRELAND'S SEVEN TRIPLE CROWNS

1894

Ireland XV v Wales: Paddy Grant (Bective); Robert Dunlop (Dublin University), Sam Lee (NIFC), Willie Gardiner (NIFC), Lucius Gwynn (Dublin University); Walter Brown (Dublin University), Ben Tuke (Bective); Andrew Bond (Derry), Tom Crean (Wanderers), Edmund Forrest (Wanderers, captain), Harry Lindsay (Dublin University), Jack Lytle (NIFC), James Lytle (NIFC), John O'Conor (Bective), Charles Rooke (Dublin University). William Sparrow (Dublin University) played at full-back against England, while George Walmsley (Bective) played for Bond in the forwards in the same game; Bertie Wells (Bective) played on the right wing against England and Scotland. **Results: 3 Feb – beat England 7-5 at Blackheath (Jack Lytle, Forrest drop-goal); 24 Feb – beat Scotland 5-0 at Lansdowne Road (Wells try, Jack Lytle conversion); 10 March – beat Wales 3-0 at Ballynafeigh, Belfast (Jack Lytle penalty)**

1899

Ireland XV v Wales: Pierce O'Brien-Butler (Monkstown); Gerald Doran (Lansdowne), George Harman (Dublin University), Carl Reid (NIFC), Edward Campbell (Monkstown); Louis Magee (London Irish and Bective, captain), Gerald Allen (Derry and Liverpool); Billy Byron (NIFC), Tommy Little (Bective), Jack McIlwaine (NIFC), Arthur Meares (Dublin University), Cecil Moriarty (Monkstown), Jack Ryan (Rockwell College), Mick Ryan (Rockwell College), Jim Sealy (Dublin University). A total of 24 players were used in the three games. After England were beaten, eight players lost their places: full-back Jack Fulton (NIFC), right wing Ian Davidson (NIFC), Harman, left wing William Brown (Dublin University) and Allen in the backs; in the pack, Tom Aherne (QCC, today UCC), Harry McCoull and McIlwaine. Harman, Allen and McIlwaine were to return six weeks later for the decider. Barnett Allison (Campbell College) at centre and forward Melville McGown (NIFC) played in the first two games, while Ainsworth Barr (Collegians) and Jack Lytle (NIFC) replaced Allen and McIlwaine for the Scotland game. **Results: 4 Feb – beat England 6-0 at Lansdowne Road (Allen try, Magee penalty); 18 Feb – beat Scotland 9-3 at Inverleith (Reid, Campbell, Sealy tries); 18 March – beat Wales 3-0 at Cardiff Arms Park (Doran try)**

1948

Ireland XV v Wales: Dudley Higgins (Civil Service, NI); Bertie O'Hanlon (Dolphin), Des McKee (NIFC), Paddy Reid (Garryowen), Barney Mullan (Clontarf); Jack Kyle (Queen's University), Ernie Strathdee (Queen's University); Bertie McConnell (Collegians), Karl Mullen (Old Belvedere, captain), Jack Daly (London Irish), Colm Callan (Lansdowne), Jimmy Nelson (Malone), Bill McKay (Queen's University), Jim McCarthy (Dolphin), Des O'Brien (London Irish). Jack Mattsson deputised for the unavailable Higgins against England; Mick O'Flanagan (Lansdowne) came in for Reid against Scotland) and Hugh de Lacy (Harlequins) started at scrum-half in the games against England and Scotland. **Results: 14 Feb – beat England 11-10 at Twickenham (Callan, Kyle and McKay tries; Mullan conversion); 28 Feb – beat Scotland 6-0 at Lansdowne Road (Mullan and Kyle tries); 13 March – beat Wales 6-3 at Ravenhill (Mullan and Daly tries)**

1949

Ireland XV v Wales: George Norton (Bective); Bertie O'Hanlon (Dolphin), Des McKee (NIFC), Noel Henderson (Queen's University), Mick Lane (UCC); Jack Kyle (Queen's University), Ernie Strathdee (Queen's University); Tom Clifford (Young Munster), Karl Mullen (Old Belvedere, captain), Leslie Griffin (Wanderers), Bob Agar (Malone), Jimmy Nelson (Malone), Bill McKay (Queen's University), Jim McCarthy (Dolphin), Des O'Brien (London Irish). Centre Tom Gavin (London Irish and Moseley) was replaced (by Henderson) after the England game, as was loose-head prop Bertie

McConnell (Collegians) and lock Colm Callan, who was replaced by Agar. **Results: 12 Feb – beat England 14-5 at Lansdowne Road (O'Hanlon and McKee tries; Norton two penalties, one conversion); 26 Feb – beat Scotland 13-3 at Murrayfield (McCarthy two tries; Norton two conversions, one penalty); 12 March – beat Wales 5-0 at St Helen's Swansea (McCarthy try, Norton conversion)**

1982

Ireland XV v Scotland: Hugo MacNeill (Dublin University); Moss Finn (Cork Con); Michael Kiernan (Dolphin), Paul Dean (St Mary's), Keith Crossan (Instonians); Ollie Campbell (Old Belvedere), Robbie McGrath (Wanderers); Phil Orr (Old Wesley), Ciaran Fitzgerald (St Mary's, captain), Gerry McLoughlin (Shannon), Moss Keane (Lansdowne), Donal Lenihan (UCC), Fergus Slattery (Blackrock College), John O'Driscoll (London Irish), Willie Duggan (Blackrock College). Again, 18 players were used over the course of the three games. Kiernan replaced David Irwin (Queen's University) because of injury during the game against Wales, while Johnny Murphy (Greystones) came on for Dean during the same game. Trevor Ringland (Queen's University) started the first two games on the right wing. **Results: 23 Jan – beat Wales 20-12 at Lansdowne Road (Finn (2) and Ringland tries; Campbell two penalties, one conversion); 6 Feb – beat England 16-15 at Twickenham (MacNeill and McLoughlin tries; Campbell two penalties, one conversion) 20 Feb – beat Scotland 21-12 at Lansdowne Road (Campbell six penalties, one drop-goal)**

1985

Ireland XV v England: Hugo MacNeill (London Irish); Trevor Ringland (Ballymena), Brendan Mullin (Dublin University), Michael Kiernan (Lansdowne), Keith Crossan (Instonians); Paul Dean (St Mary's College), Michael Bradley (Cork Con); Phil Orr (Old Wesley), Ciaran Fitzgerald (St Mary's College, captain), Jim McCoy (Dungannon), Willie Anderson (Dungannon), Donal Lenihan (Cork Con), Philip Matthews (Ards), Nigel Carr (Ards) Brian Spillane (Bohemians). The same 15 players began and ended all three games. **Results: 2 Feb – beat Scotland 18-15 at Murrayfield (Ringland two tries; Kiernan, two penalties, one conversion and a drop-goal); 16 March – beat Wales 21-9 at Cardiff Arms Park (Ringland, Crossan tries; Kiernan three penalties, two conversions); 30 March – beat England 13-10 at Lansdowne Road (Mullin try; Kiernan two penalties, one drop-goal).**

2004

Ireland XV v Scotland: Girvan Dempsey (Leinster/Terenure College); Shane Horgan (Leinster/Lansdowne), Gordon D'Arcy (Leinster/Lansdowne), Brian O'Driscoll (Leinster/Blackrock College, captain), Geordan Murphy (Leicester); Ronan O'Gara (Munster/Cork Con), Peter Stringer (Munster/Shannon); Reggie Corrigan (Leinster/Greystones), Shane Byrne (Leinster/Blackrock College), John Hayes (Munster/Shannon), Malcolm O'Kelly (Leinster/St Mary's College), Paul O'Connell (Munster/Young Munster), Simon Easterby (Llanelli), David Wallace (Munster/Garryowen), Anthony Foley (Munster/Shannon). Tyrone Howe (Ulster and Dungannon) played on the left wing against Wales and England, while Keith Gleeson (Leinster and St Mary's College) played at open-side flanker in the same games. Donncha O'Callaghan started in place of O'Kelly against Wales, while seven other players appeared as replacements during the course of the three games: Kevin Maggs (Bath), David Humphreys (Ulster/Dungannon), Guy Easterby (Rotherham), Marcus Horan (Munster/Shannon), Simon Best (Ulster/Belfast Harlequins), Frankie Sheahan (Munster/Cork Con) and Victor Costello (Leinster/St Mary's). **Results: 22 Feb – beat Wales 36-15 at Lansdowne Road (Byrne and O'Driscoll two tries each, O'Gara and Foley tries; O'Gara three conversions); 6 March – beat England 19-13 at Twickenham (Dempsey try; O'Gara four penalties, one conversion); 27 March – beat Scotland 37-16 at Lansdowne Road (D'Arcy two tries; Murphy, Wallace, Stringer tries; O'Gara two penalties, two conversions)**